A LOOK INTO

AFRICAN ART
Oceanic Art

Conceived, Designed, and Illustrated by:
Mrinal Mitra

Series edited by:
Swarna Mitra & Malika Mitra

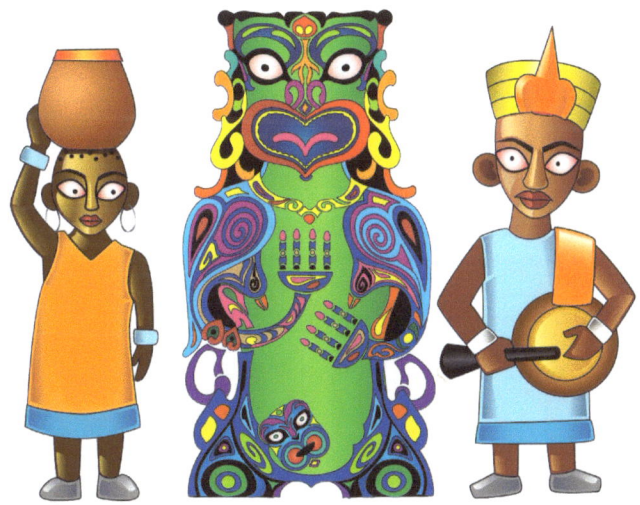

This series is dedicated to the citizens of the world;
from the young blooming minds of children, to the aspired individuals of all ages.

THE WORLD CULTURE ART
VOLUME-1

A **LOOK** INTO
AFRICAN ART

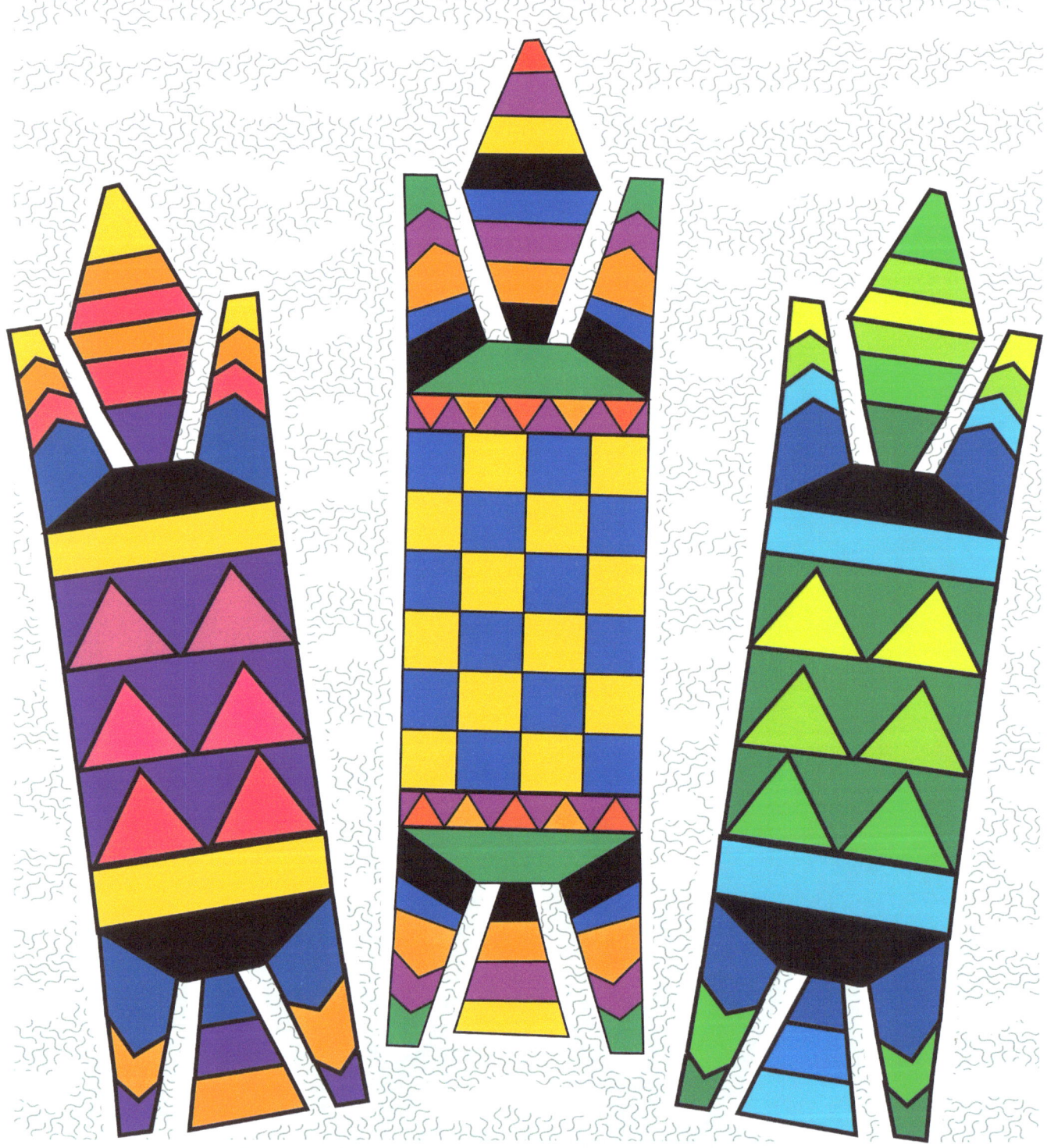

Part of a dance mask from Do the Guardian Spirit.
Bobo, Upper Volta (Burkina Faso). These masks are worn by
groups of youth after sowing.

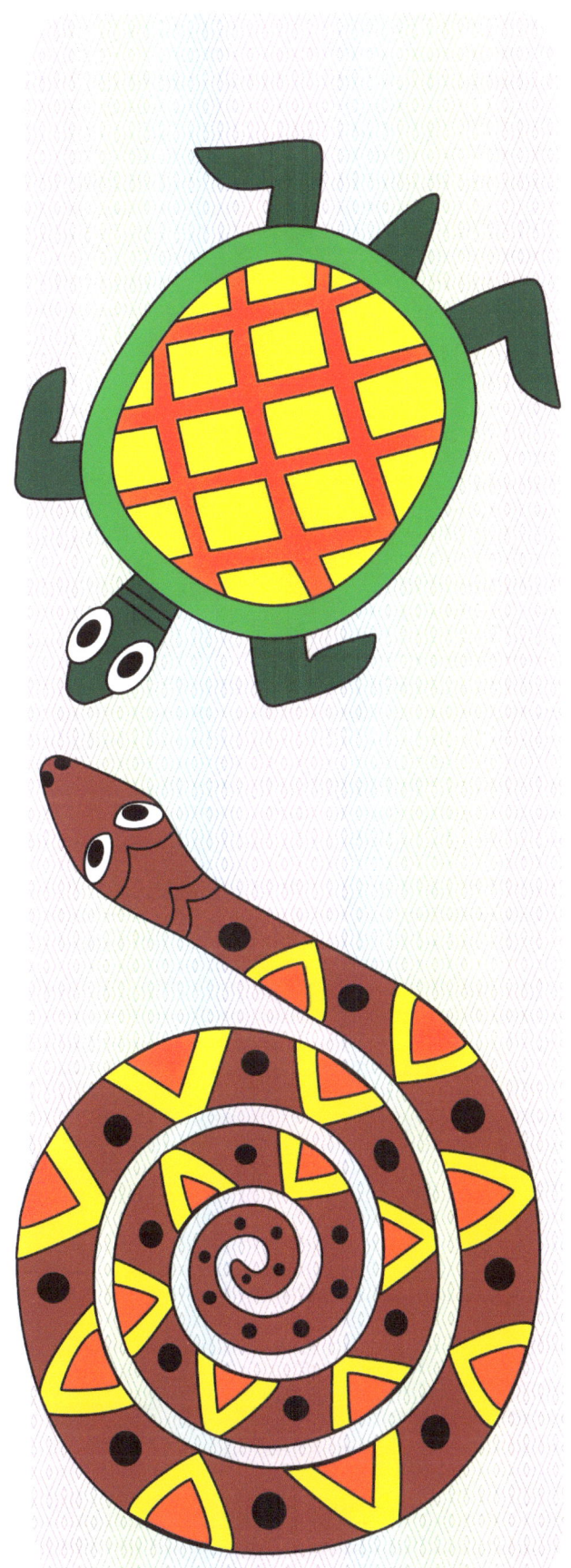

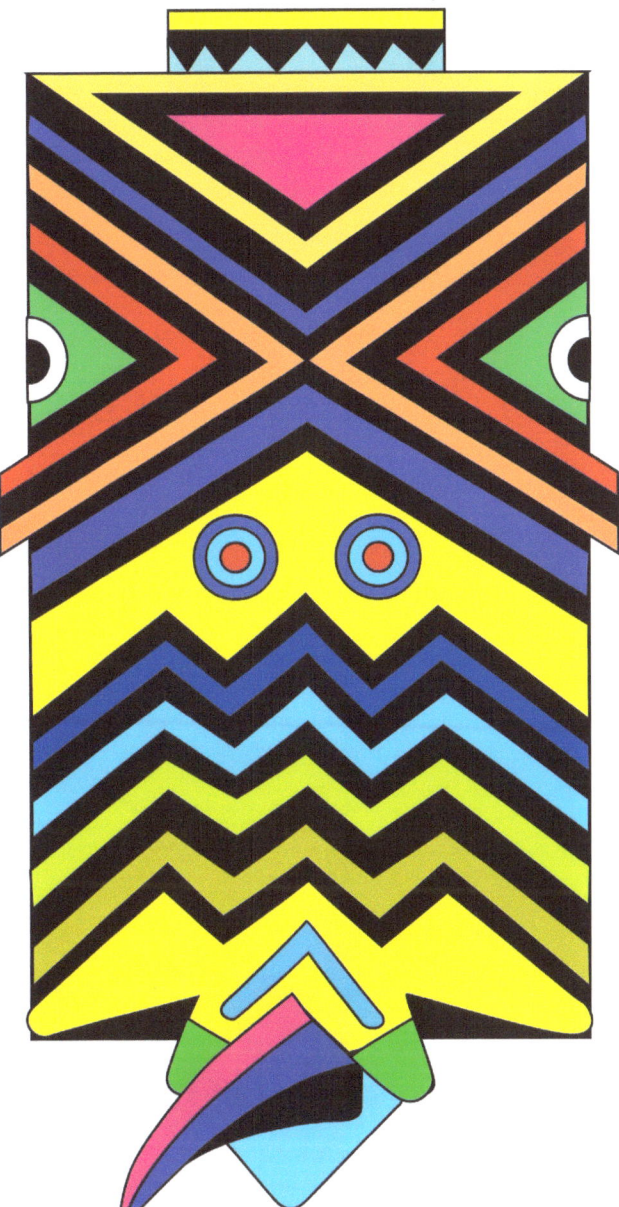

Bird mask. Wood.
Bobo, Dioulasso region.
Upper Volta (Barkina Faso).

Coiled snake and turtle on a frieze found
in a palace door in Yoruba, Nigeria.

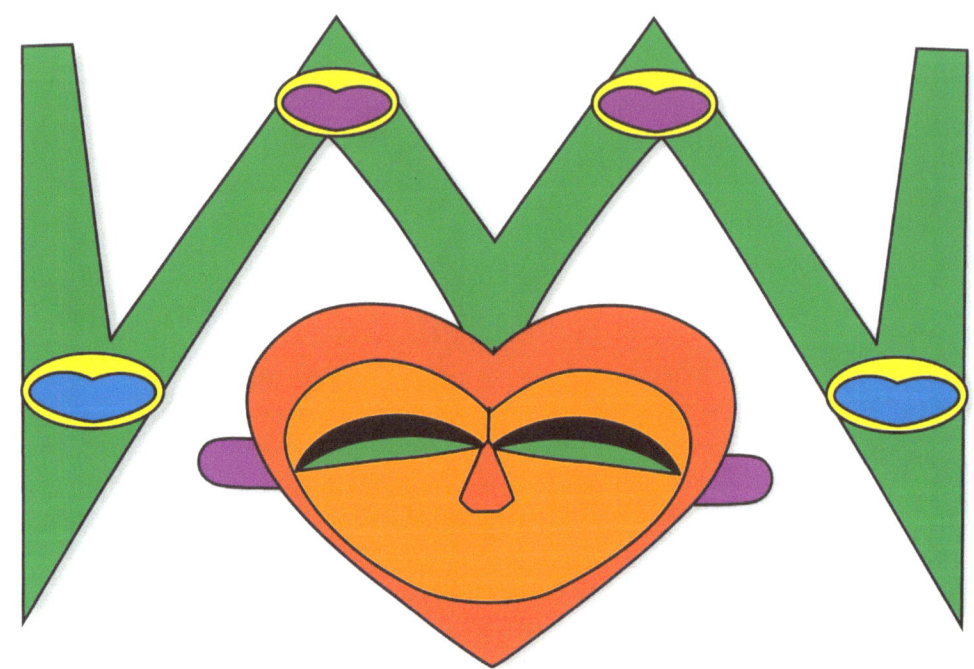

Dance mask, from Bakwele. Woodwork. Congo.

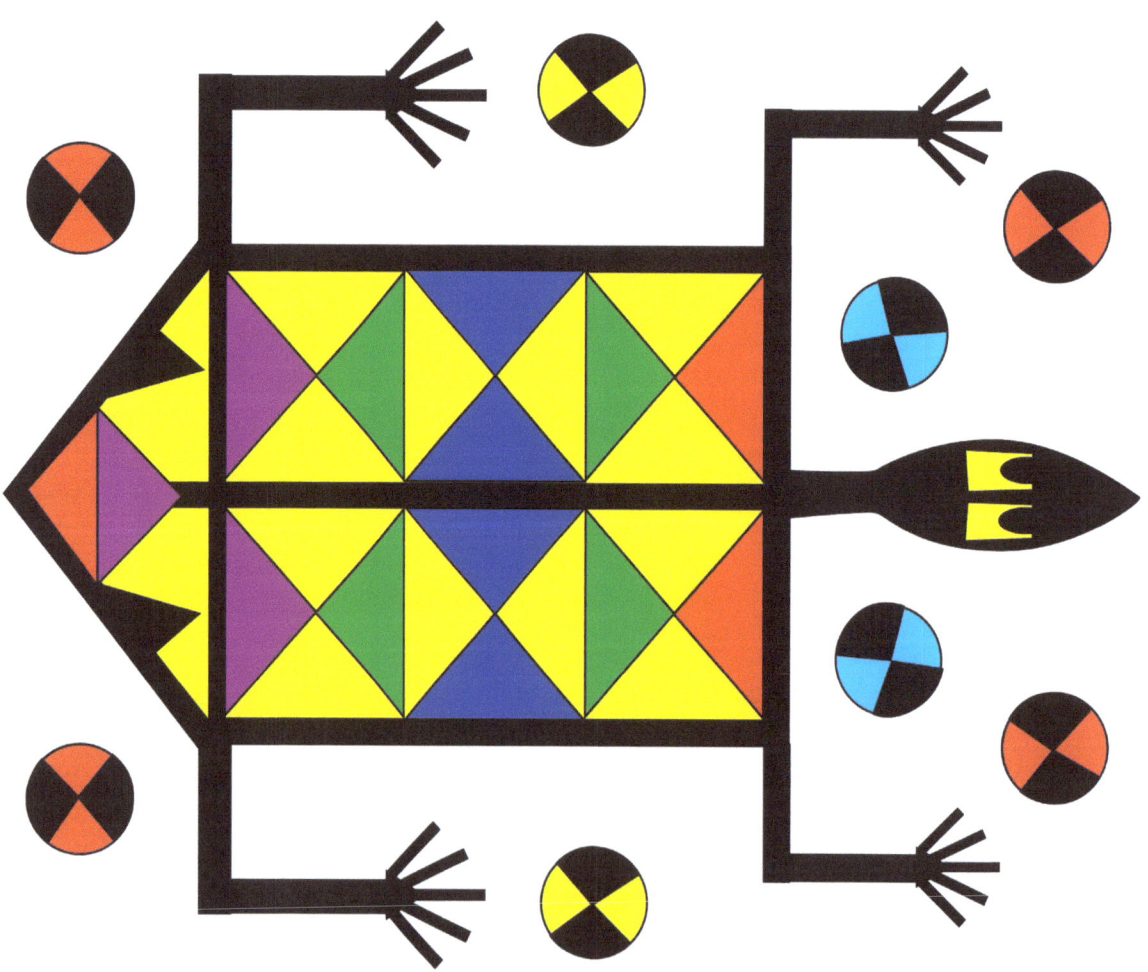

Hand painted Senufo cloth showing wild animal. Cote d'Ivoire (Ivory Coast).

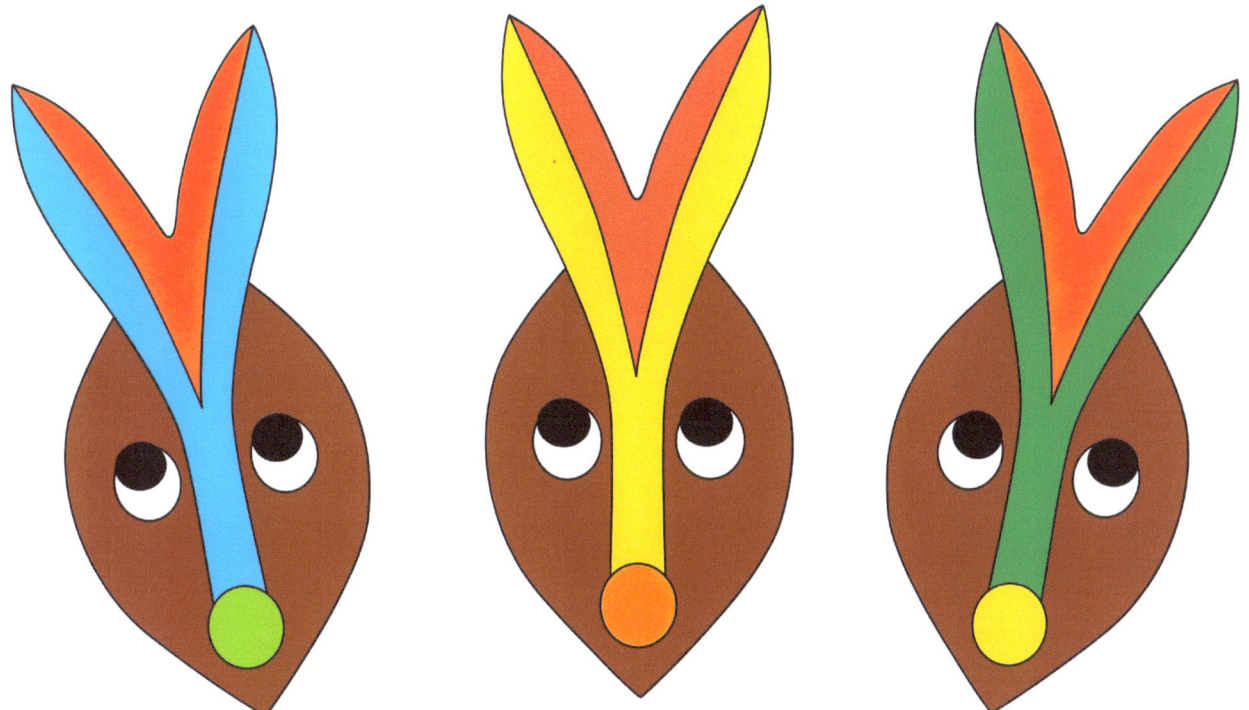

Karikpo mask. Ogoni, Southern Nigeria.
This mask is worn when dancing at the
farming season for the local deity.

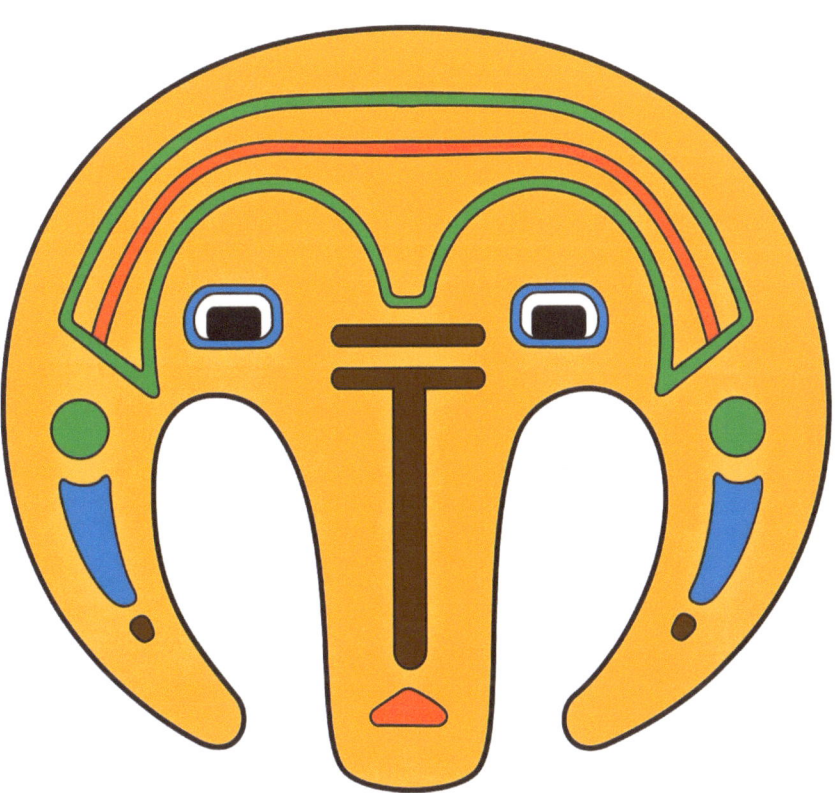

Ornamental fetish mask. Cote d'Ivoire (Ivory Coast).

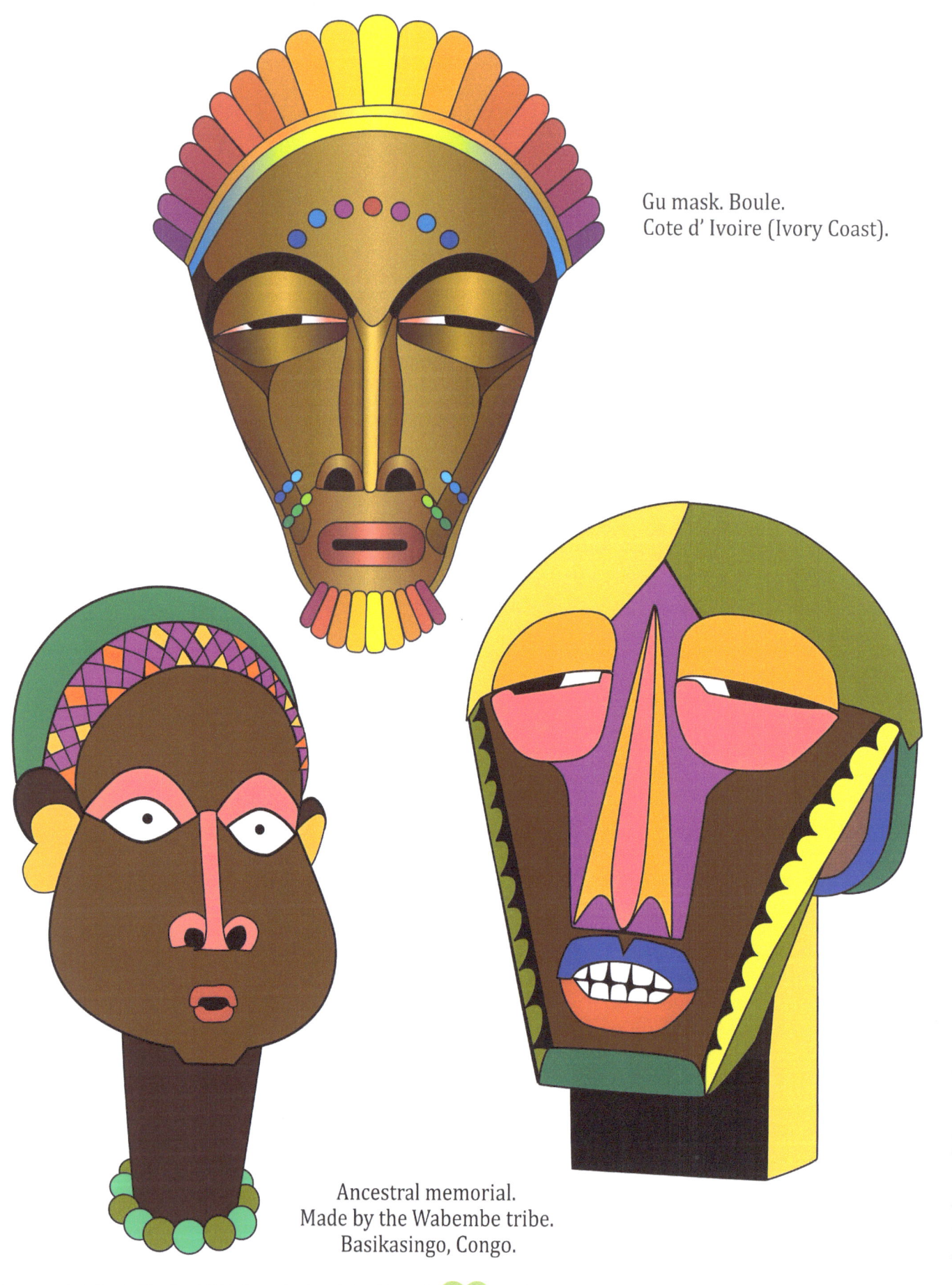

Gu mask. Boule.
Cote d' Ivoire (Ivory Coast).

Ancestral memorial.
Made by the Wabembe tribe.
Basikasingo, Congo.

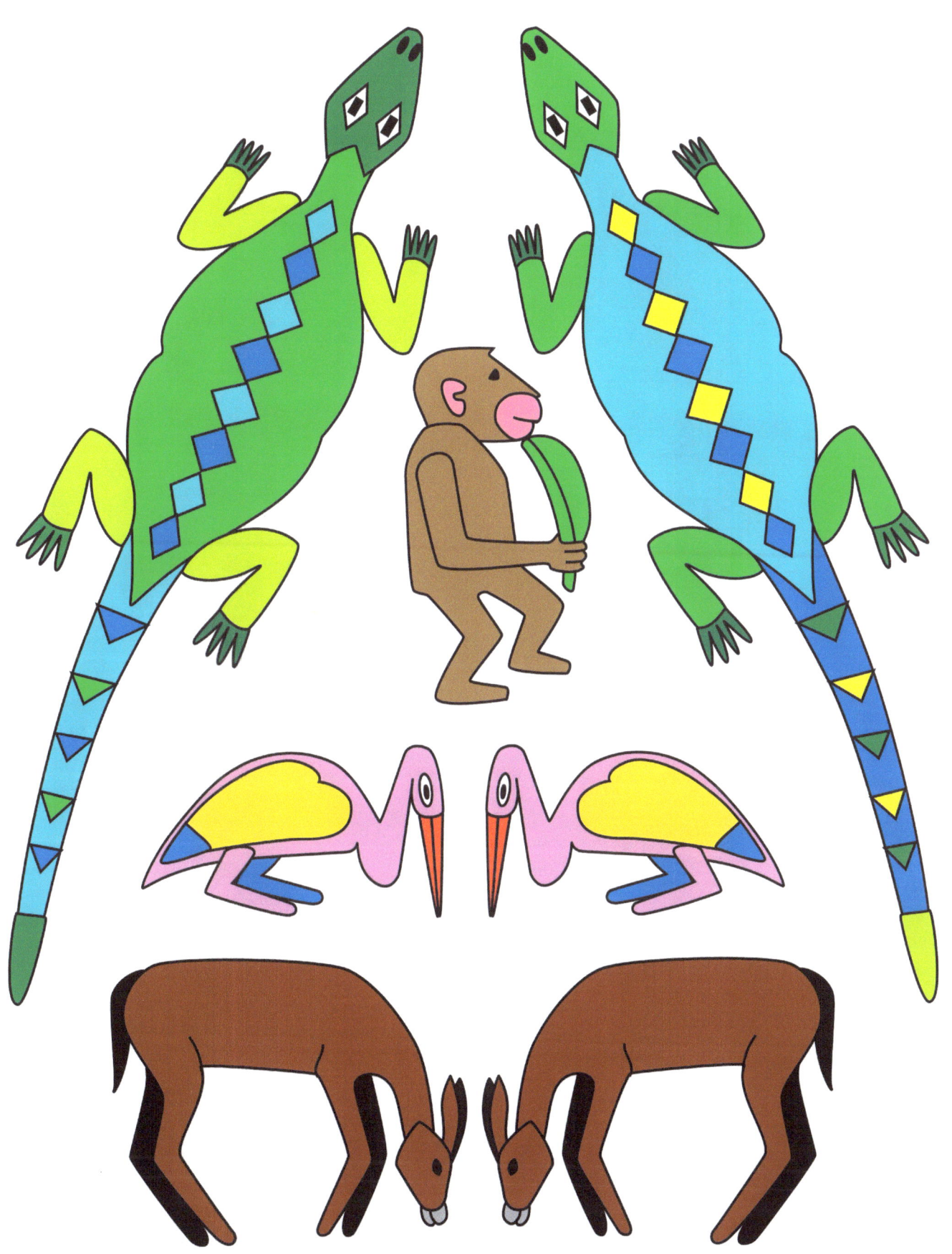

Animal motifs from a granary door, Senufo. Woodwork. Northern Cote d'Ivoire (Ivory Coast).

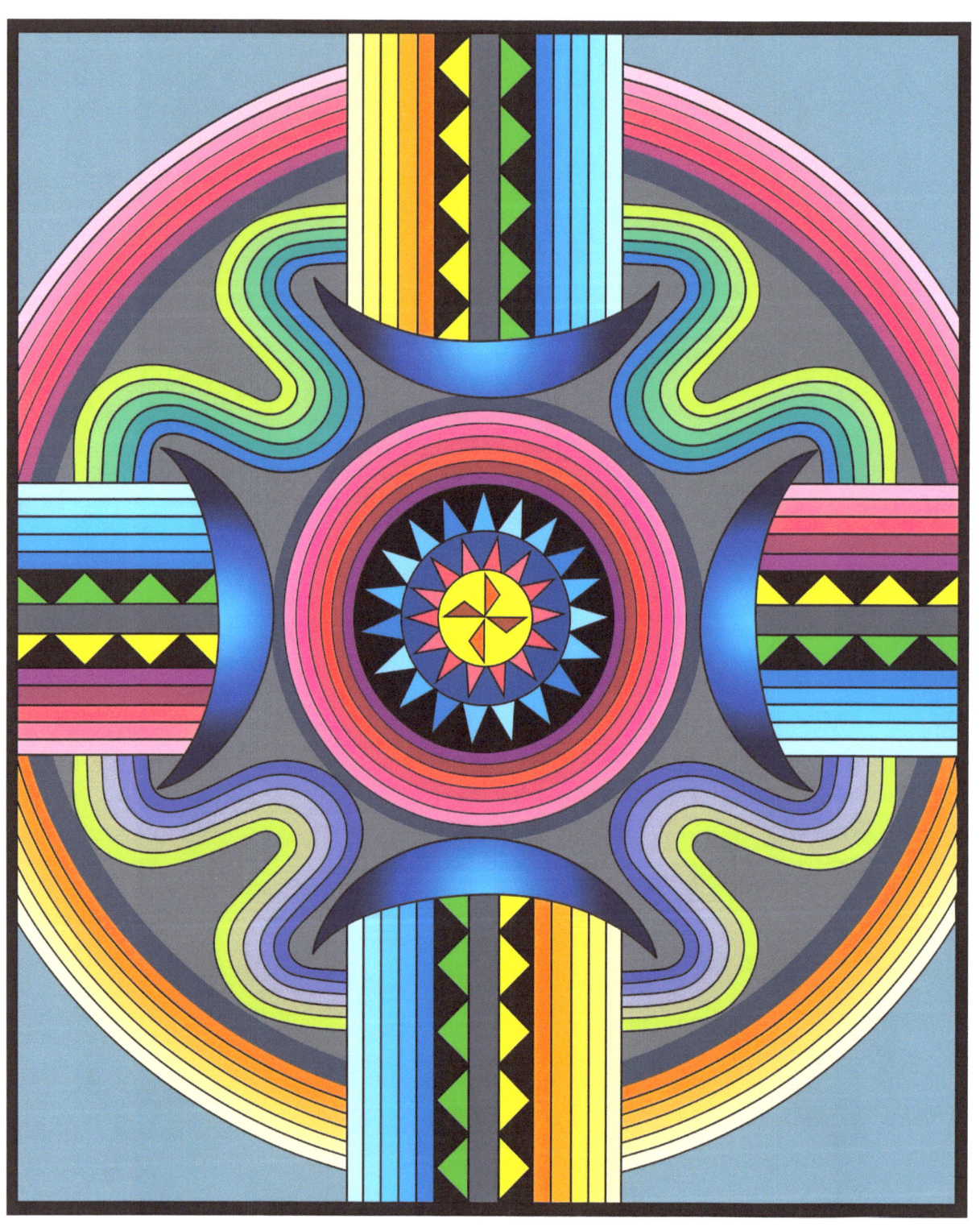

Designs and patterns are woven in silk Kente Cloth. Ashanti, Ghana.

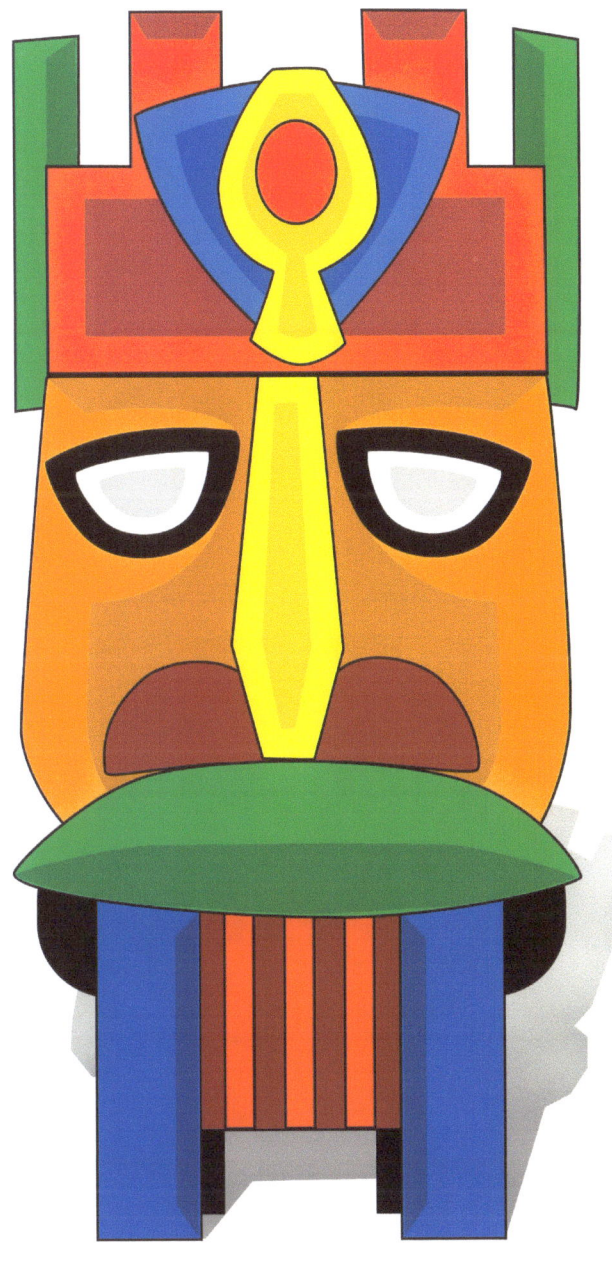

Mask of the Water Spirit.
Woodwork. Nigeria.

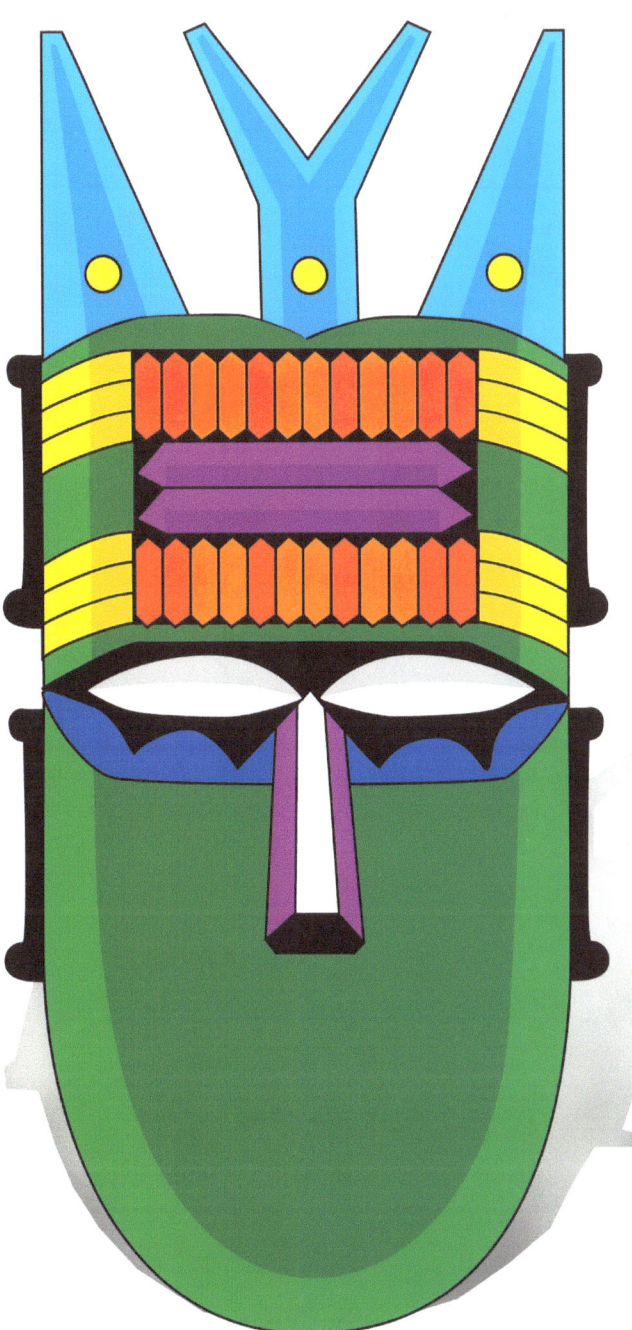

Mask of the Poro Society.
Woodwork. Toma, Guinea Coast.

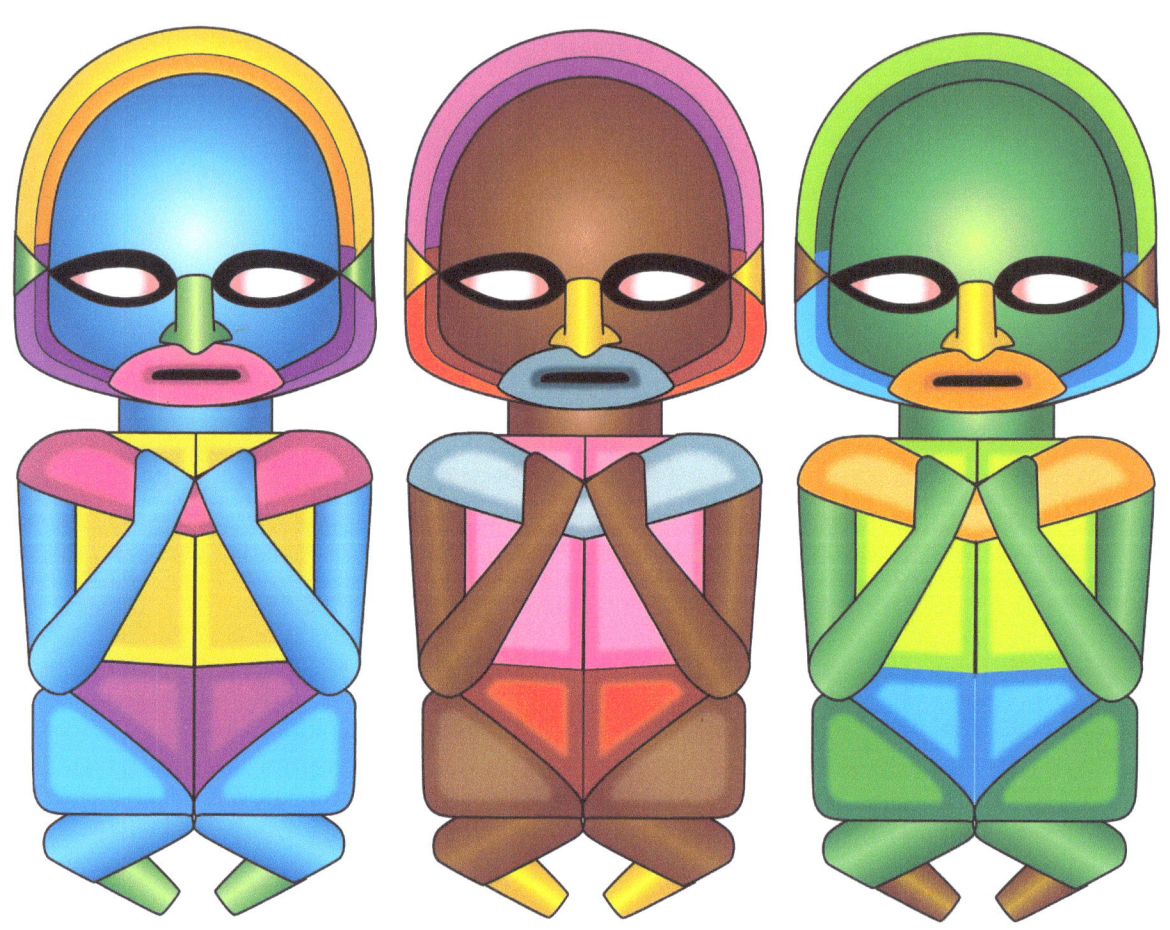

Initiation amulet. Woodwork. Bahungana, Congo.

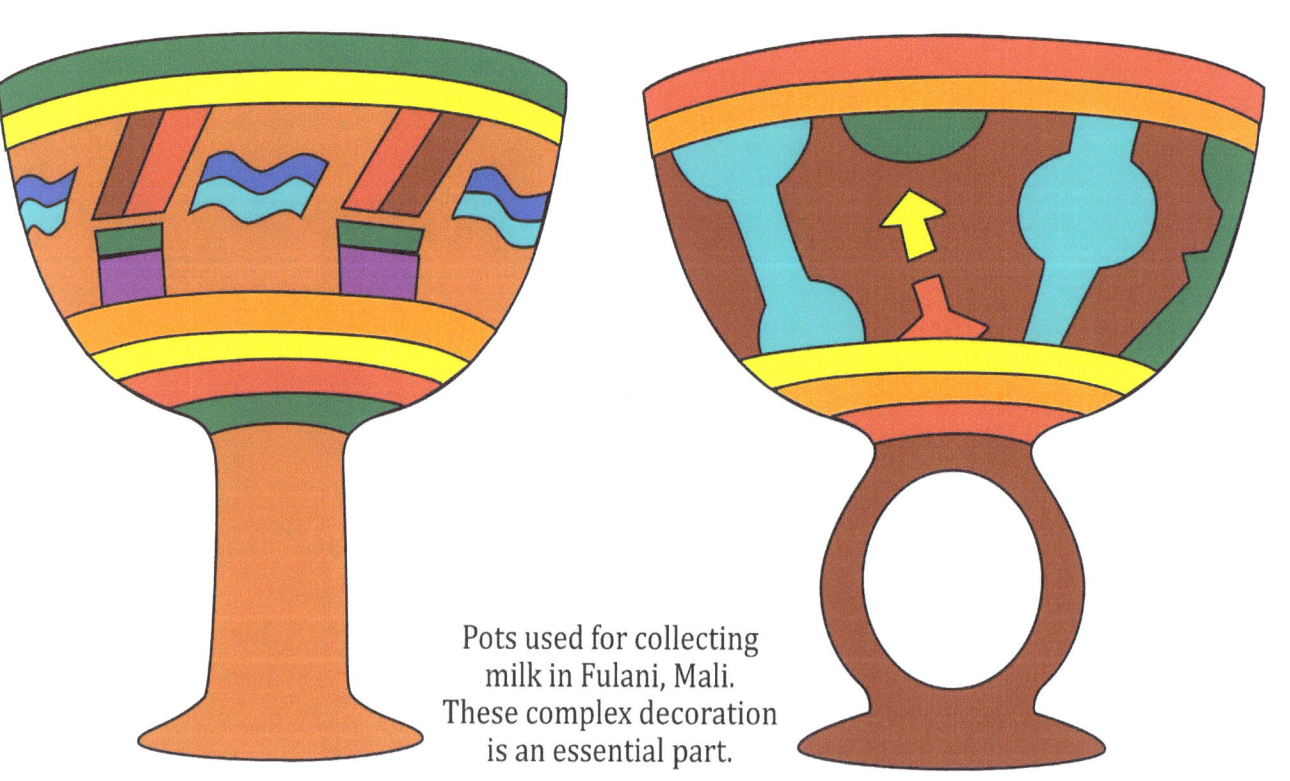

Pots used for collecting
milk in Fulani, Mali.
These complex decoration
is an essential part.

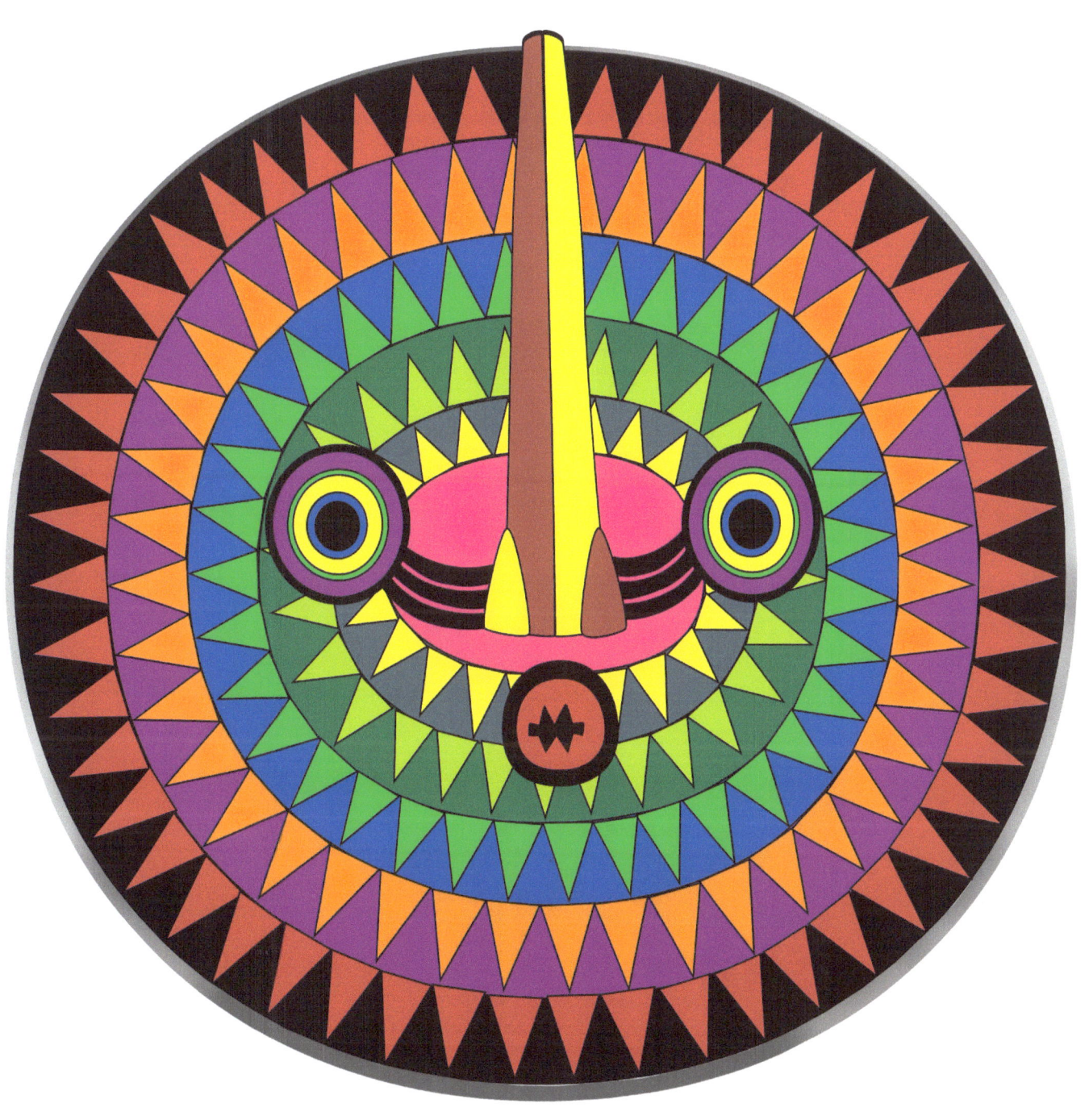

The Bobo population from Burkina Faso, Africa, carve circular masks like this on wood to represent owls and other birds. These masks are worn for performative rituals.

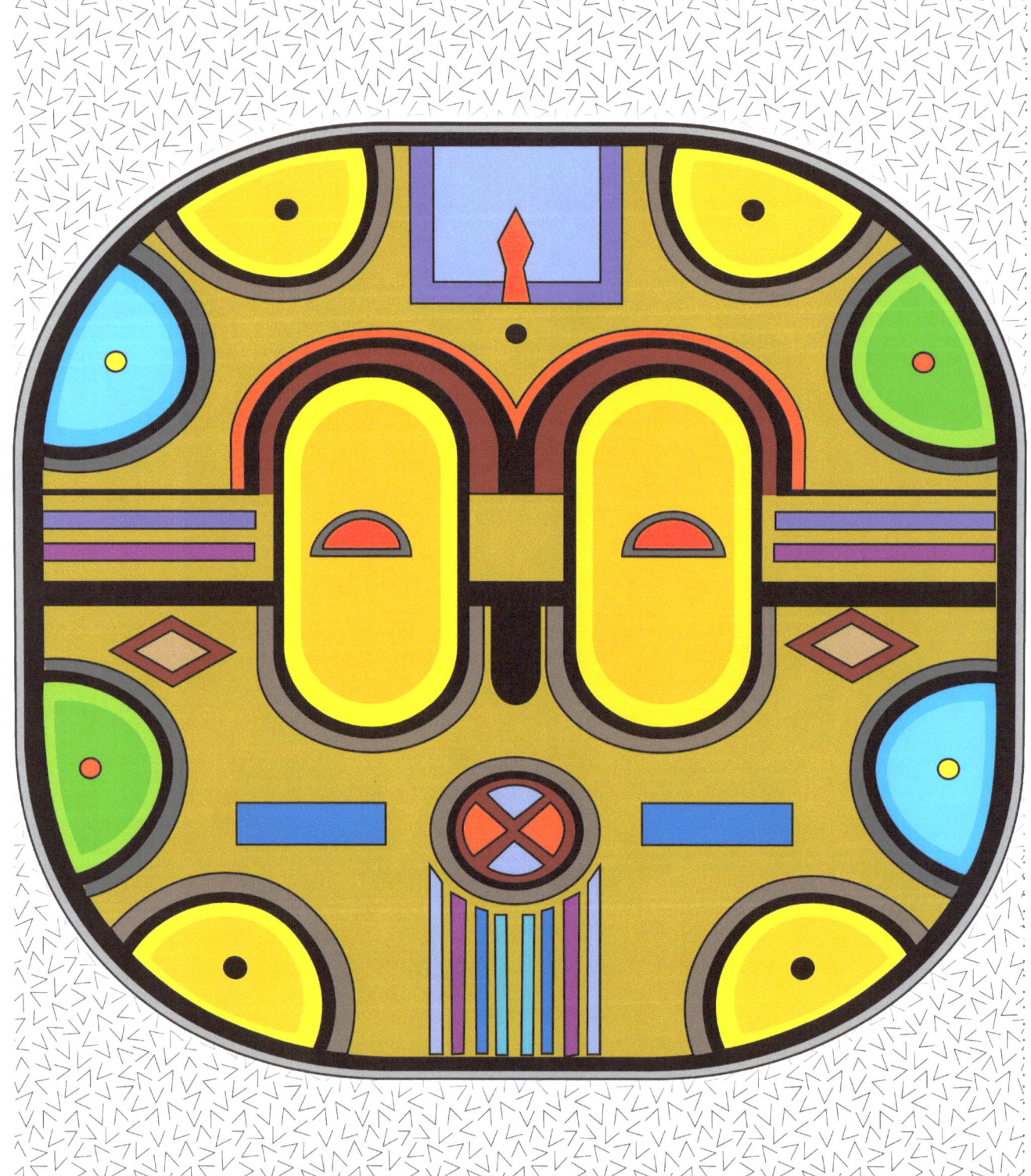

Teke Mask, from the Teke tribe of Congo. Hand carved on wood.
An abstraction of the human face. The nose and ear are prominent.

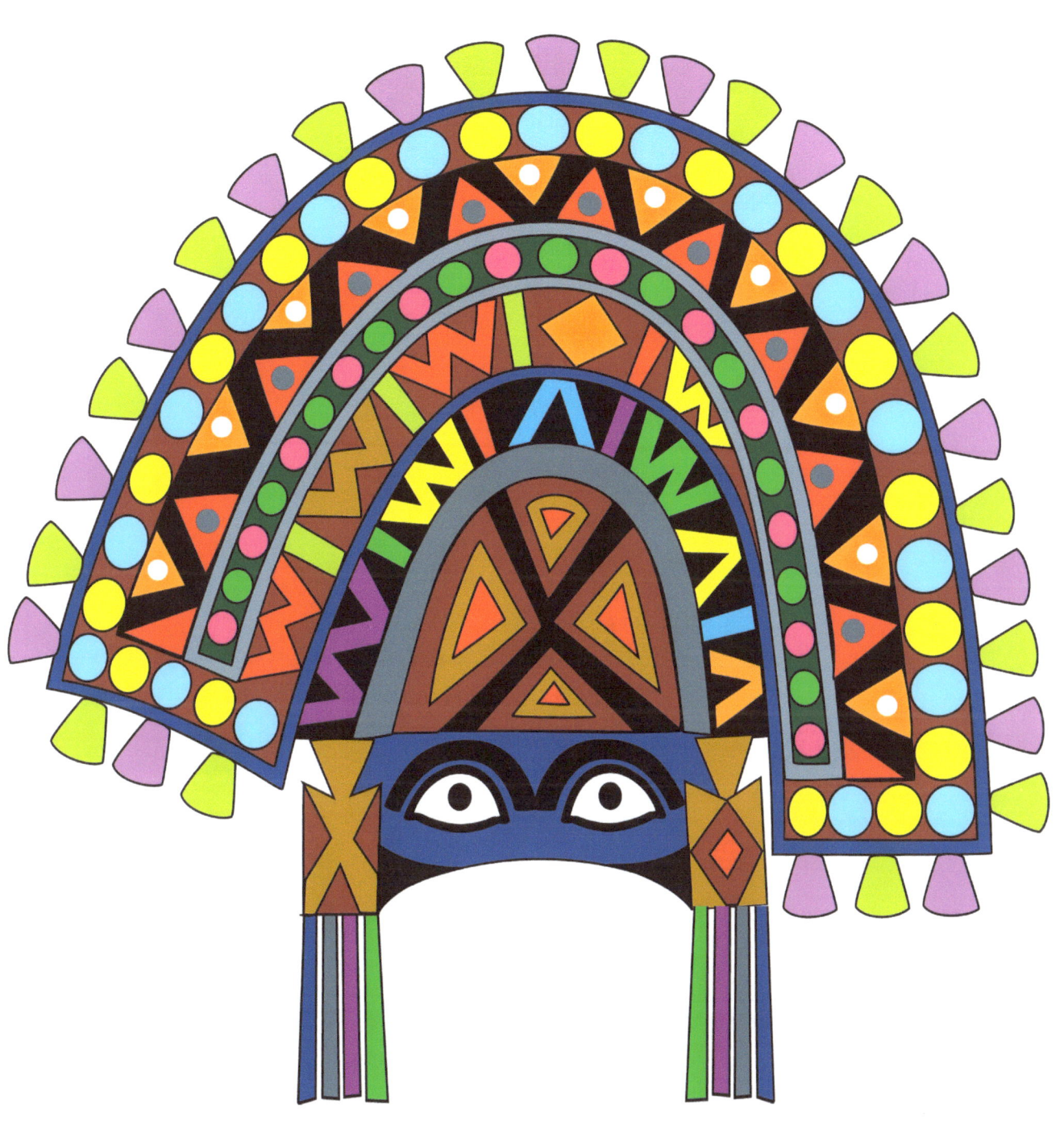

Part of a Crested mask of the
Mmwo Society (cult of the female ancestral spirits), Igbo (Ibo). Woodwork. Nigeria.

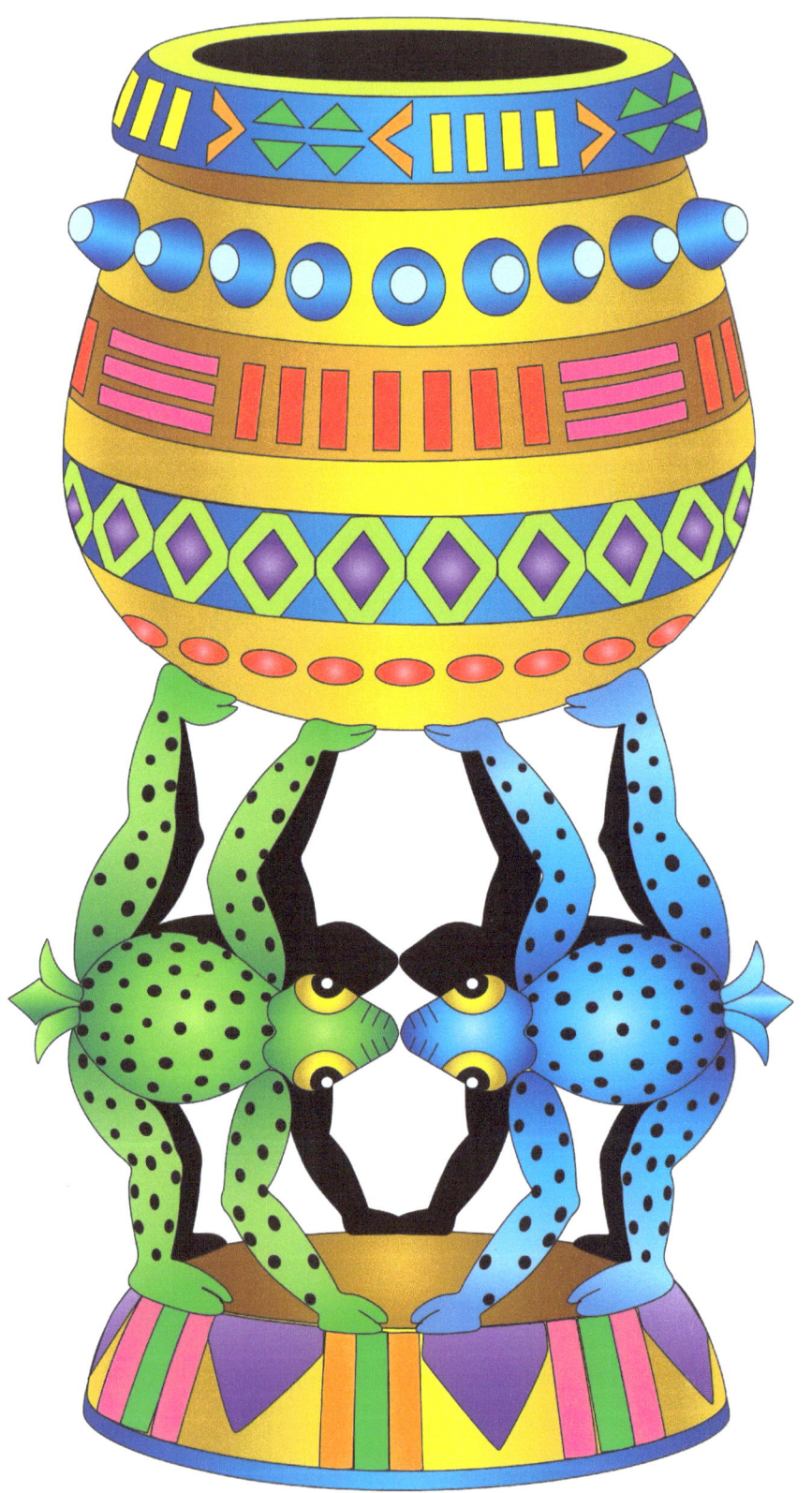

Oracle Bowl
Used to perform rituals, and to worship ancestors by societies of Yoruba, Nigeria, and Mali.

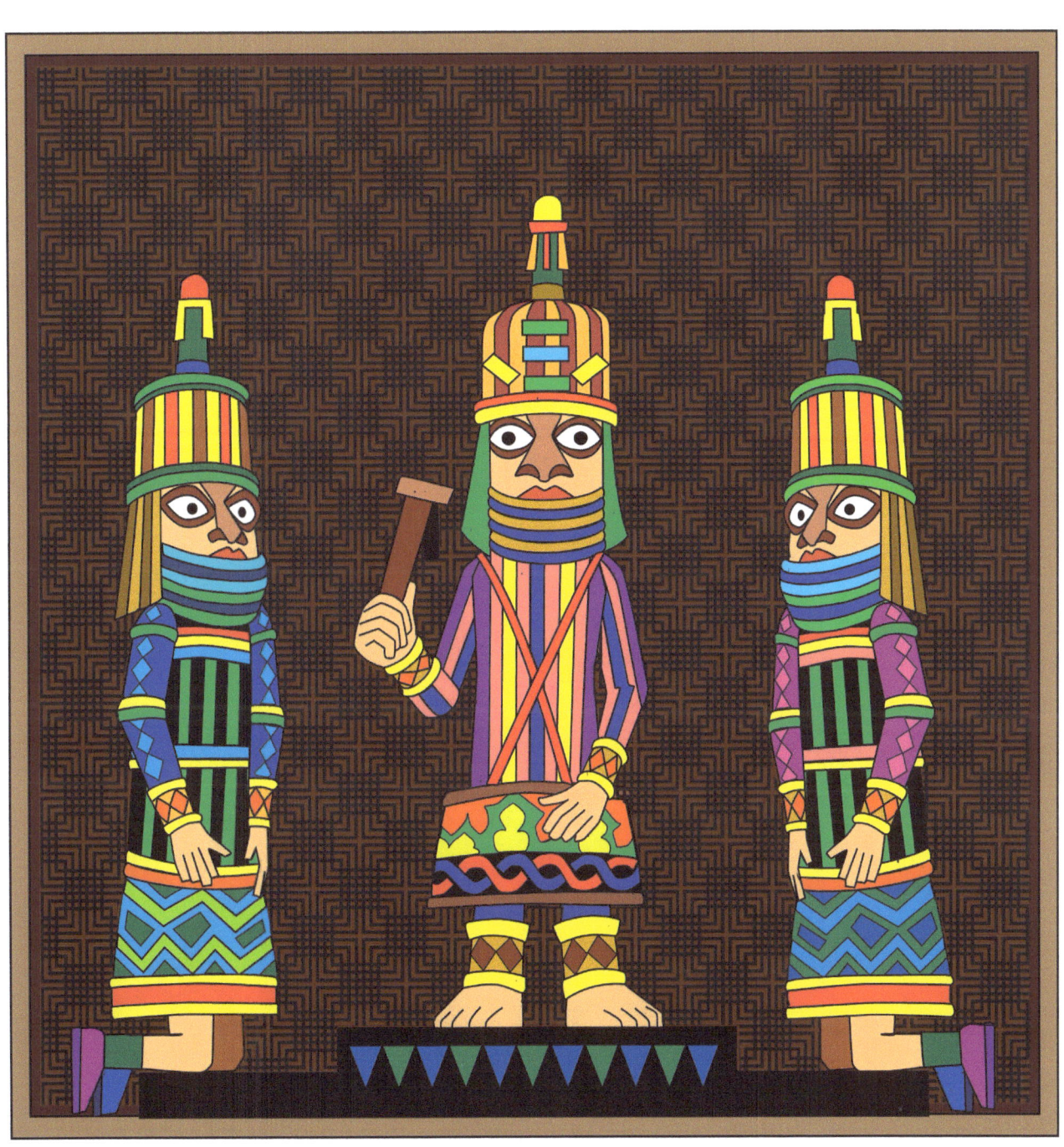

Bronze Plaque, Benin, Nigeria. Made by Oba's special
craftsmen to set forth his glory and power. 17th Century C.E.

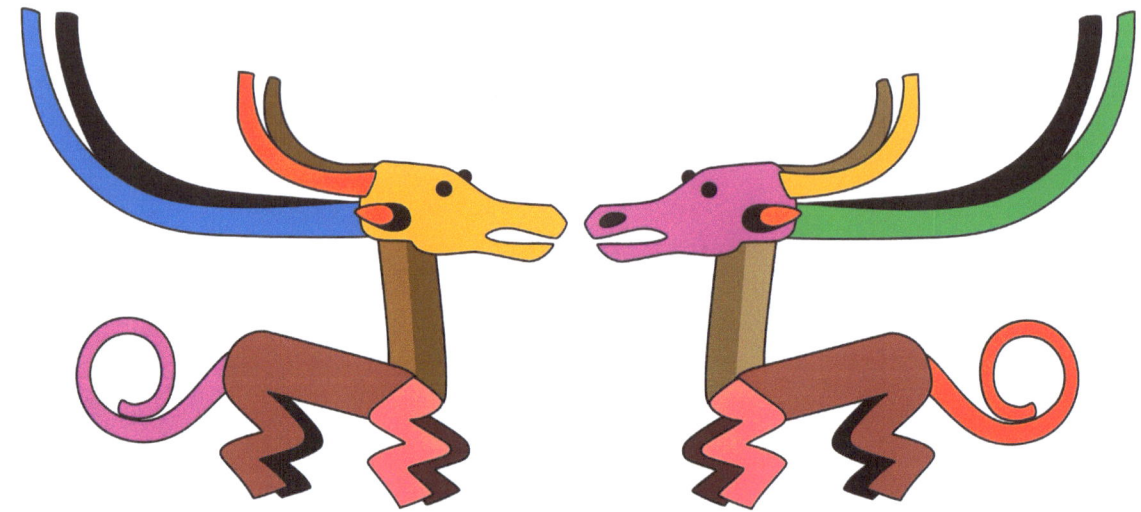

Chi-wara dance headdress. Bambara, Mali. Long sweeping horns that are parallel to their backs, gave a charming appeal..

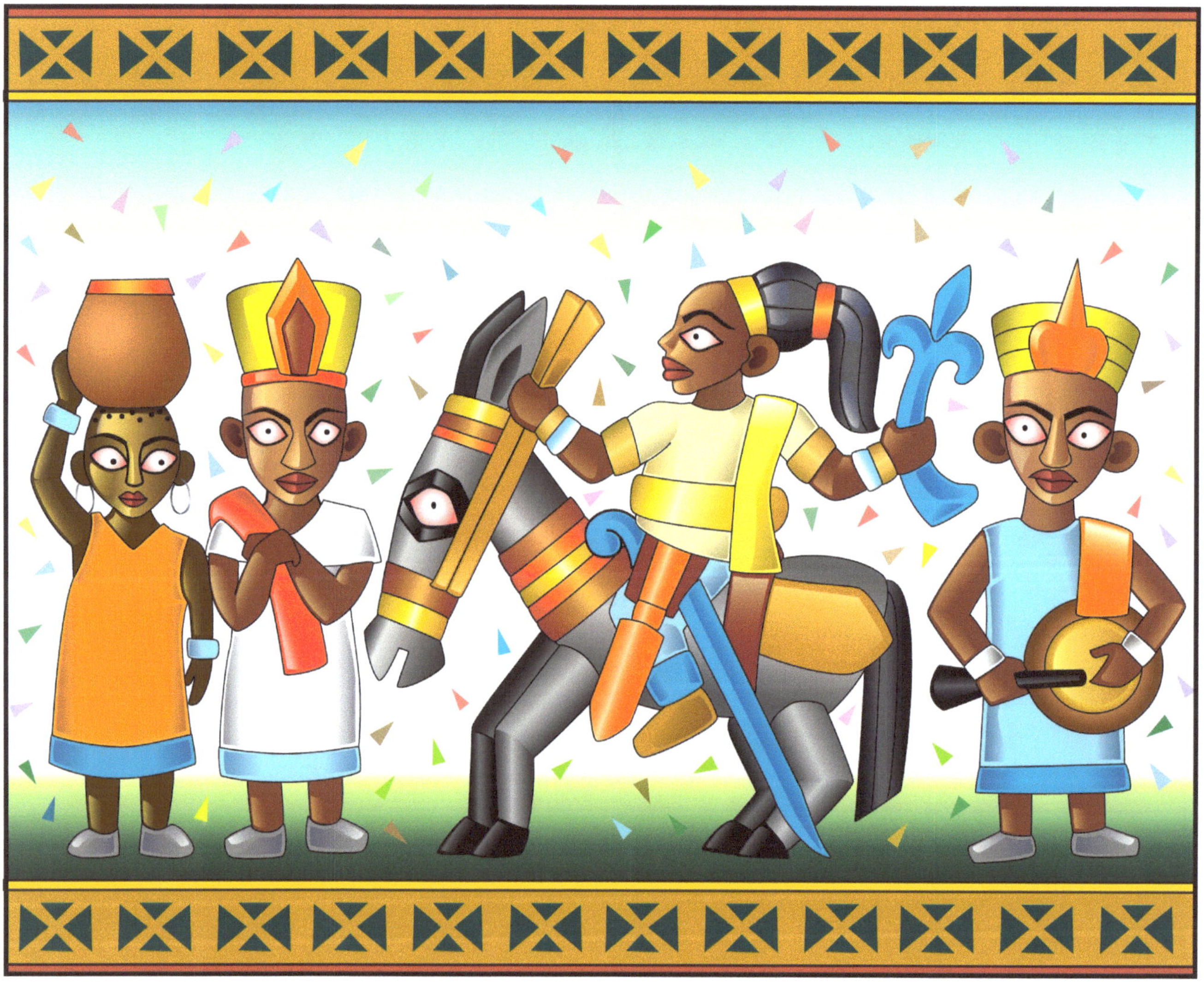

Part of a Royal Procession from the frieze in the palace door in Yoruba, Nigeria.

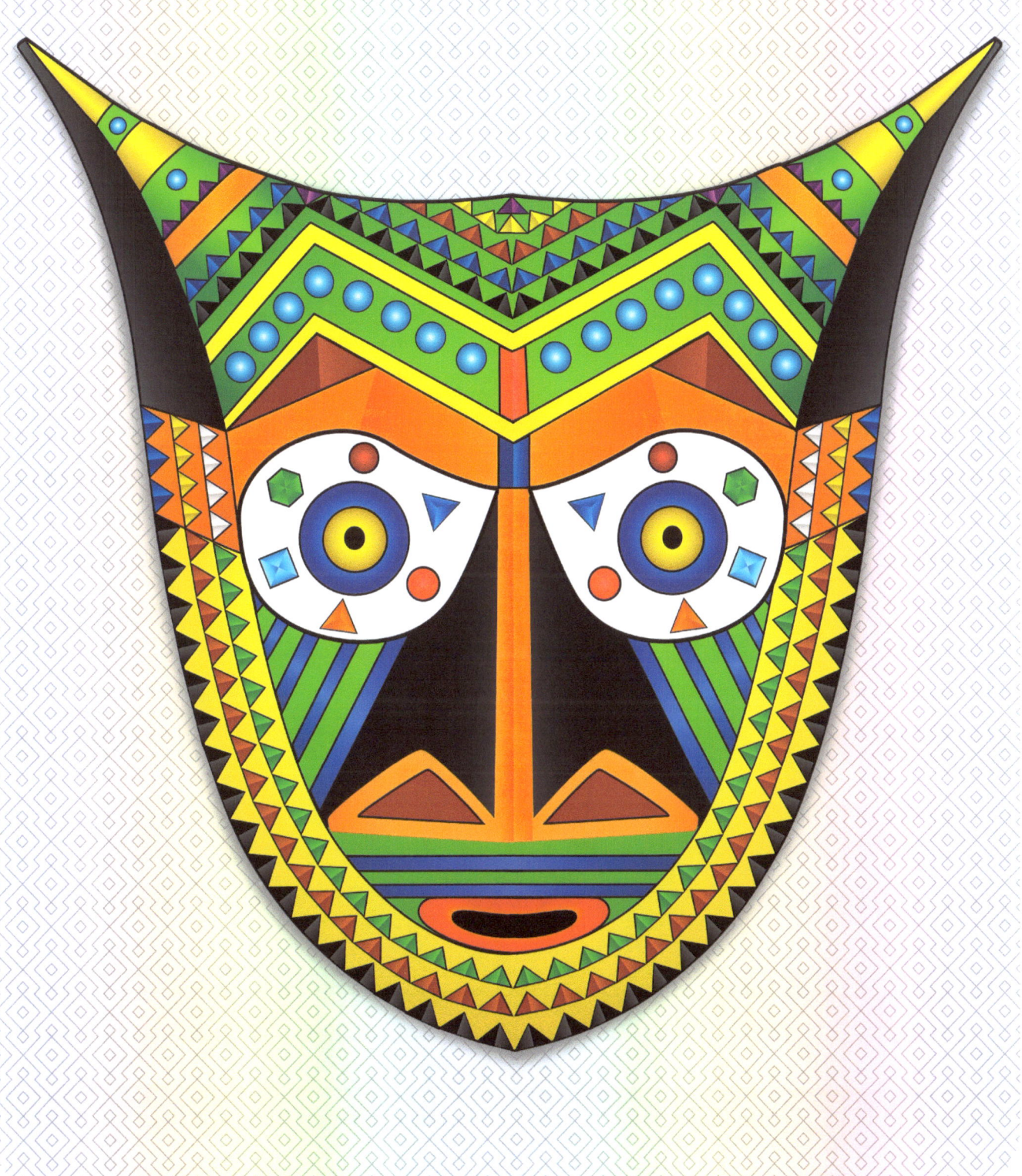

Dance mask, woodwork. Bakuba, Democratic Republic of the Congo.

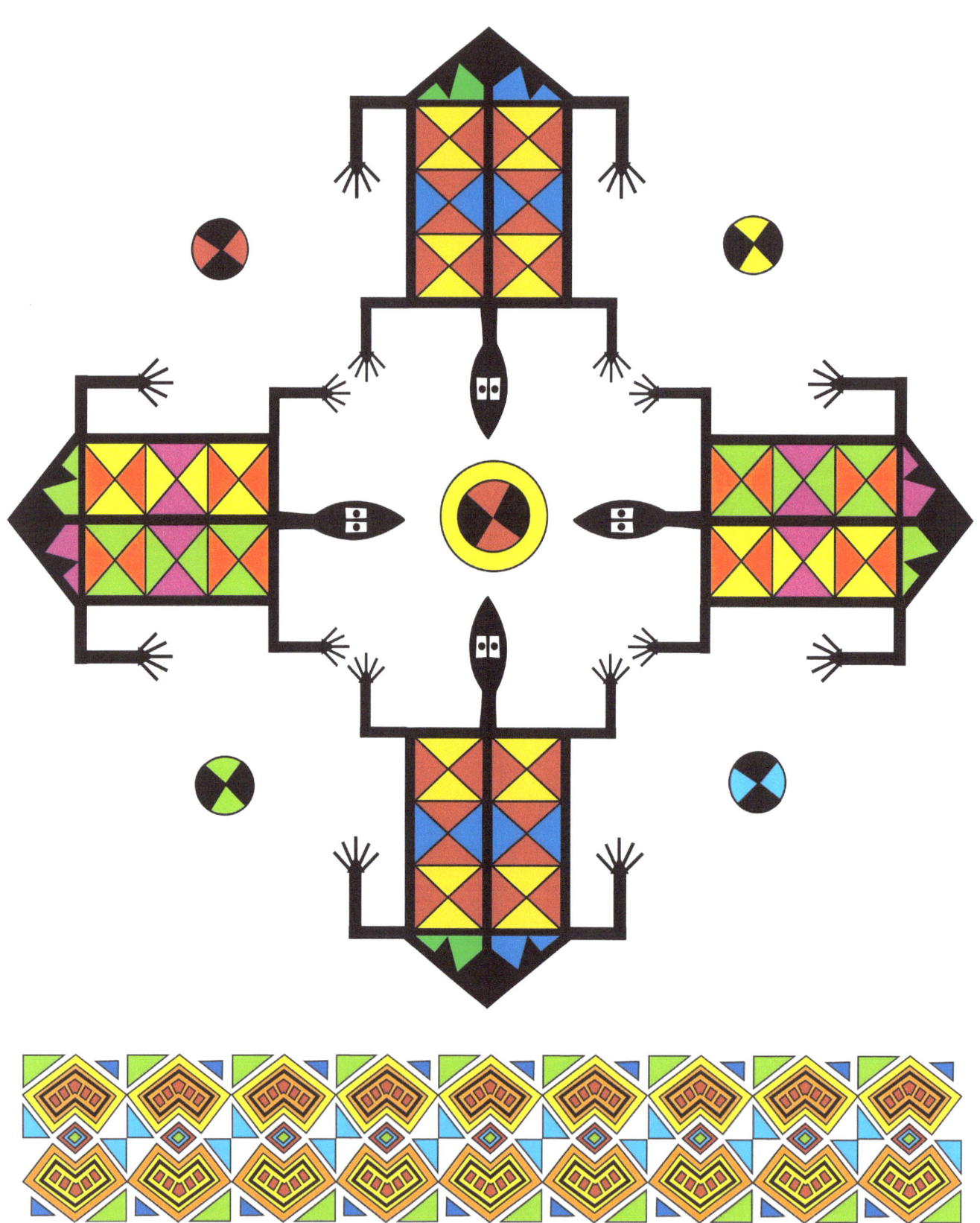

Examples of images created using the elements found in African Art

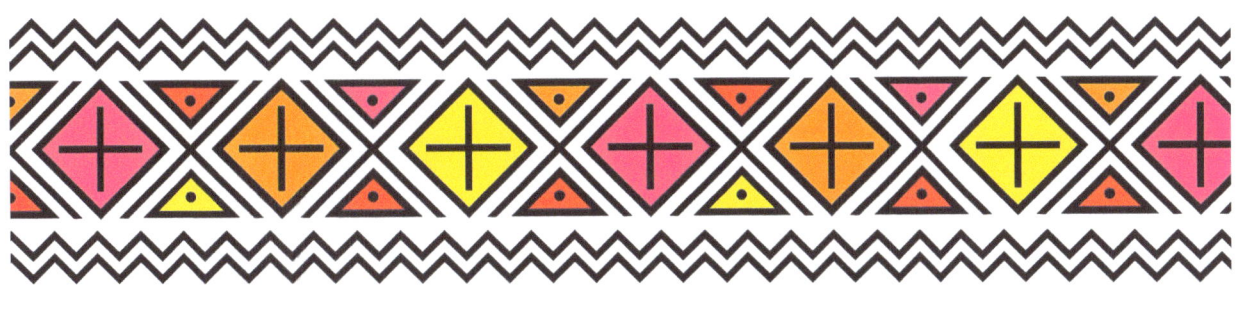

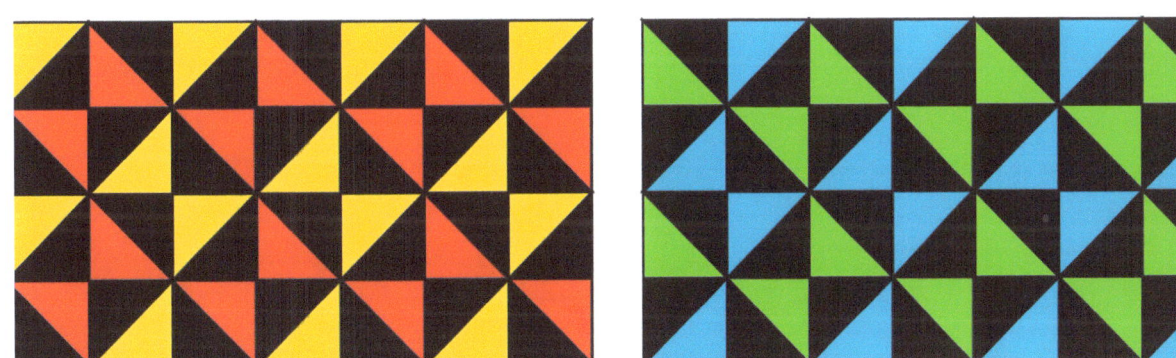

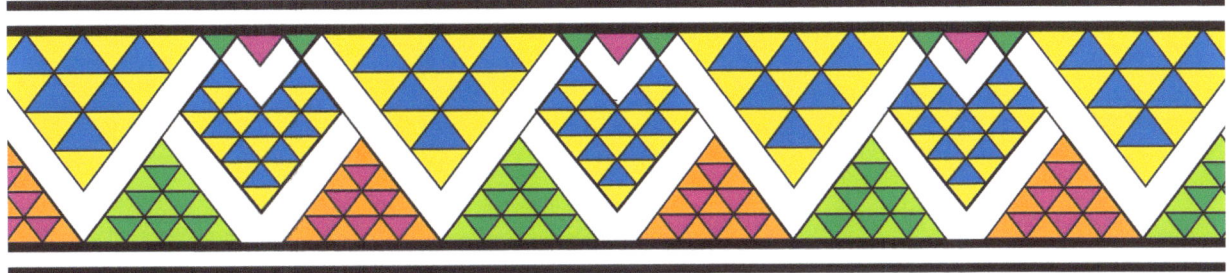

Examples of images created using the elements found in African Art

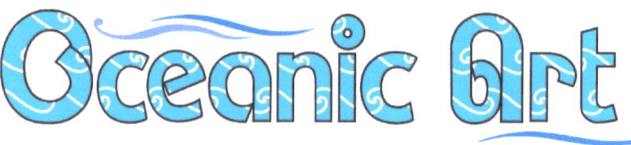

Oceanic Art

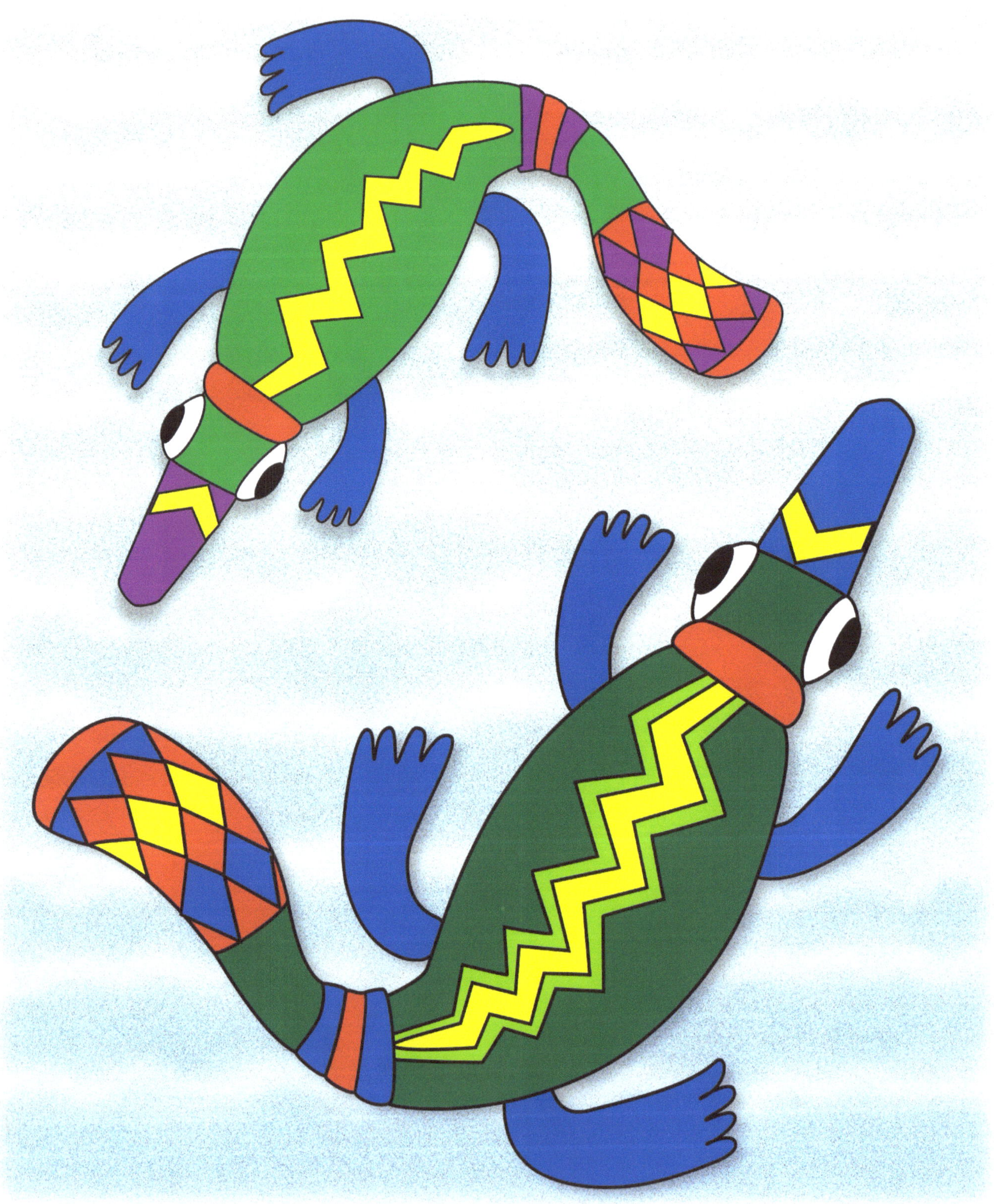

Highly stylized crocodile on a house panel with relief. Maori woodwork. New Zealand.

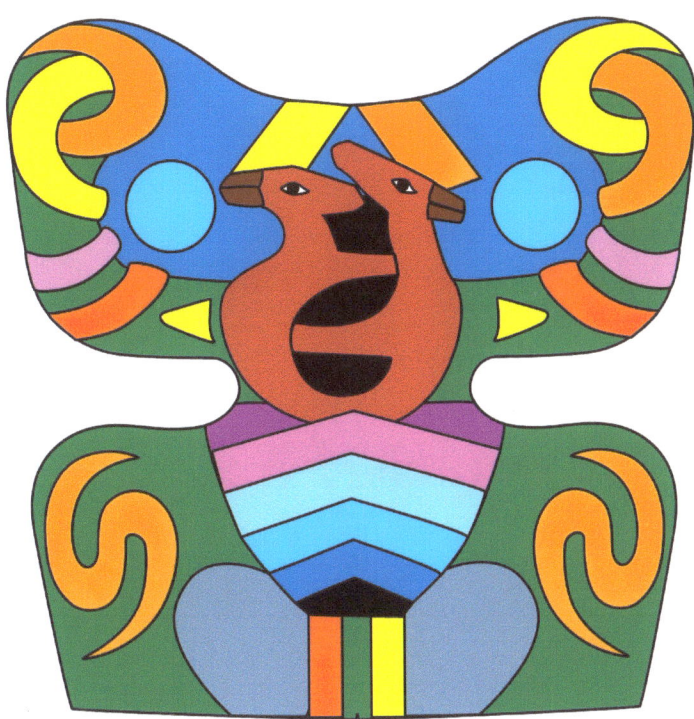

On a house panel with relief woodwork. Maori art. New Zealand.

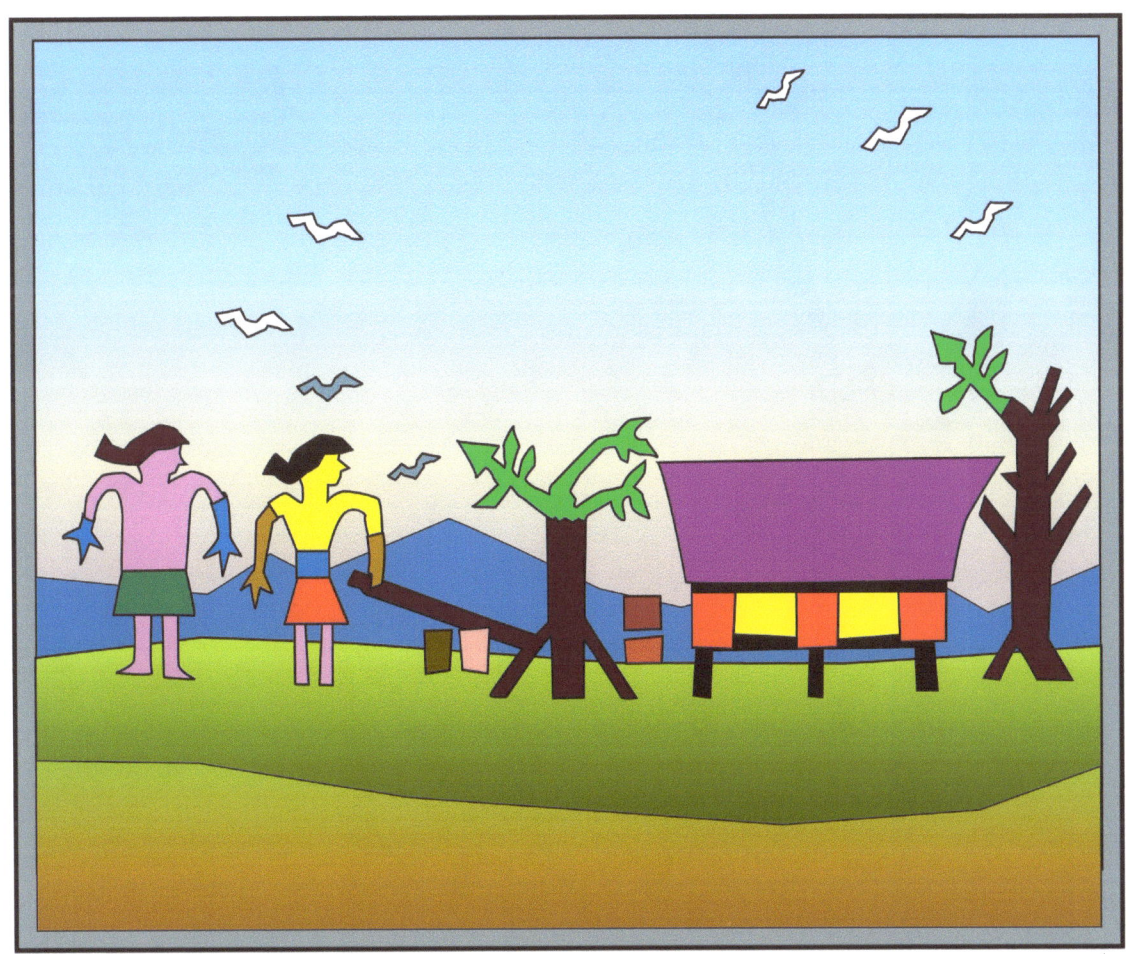

A relief carving on the beam of a bachelor's house from the Palau Island, Maori woodwork.

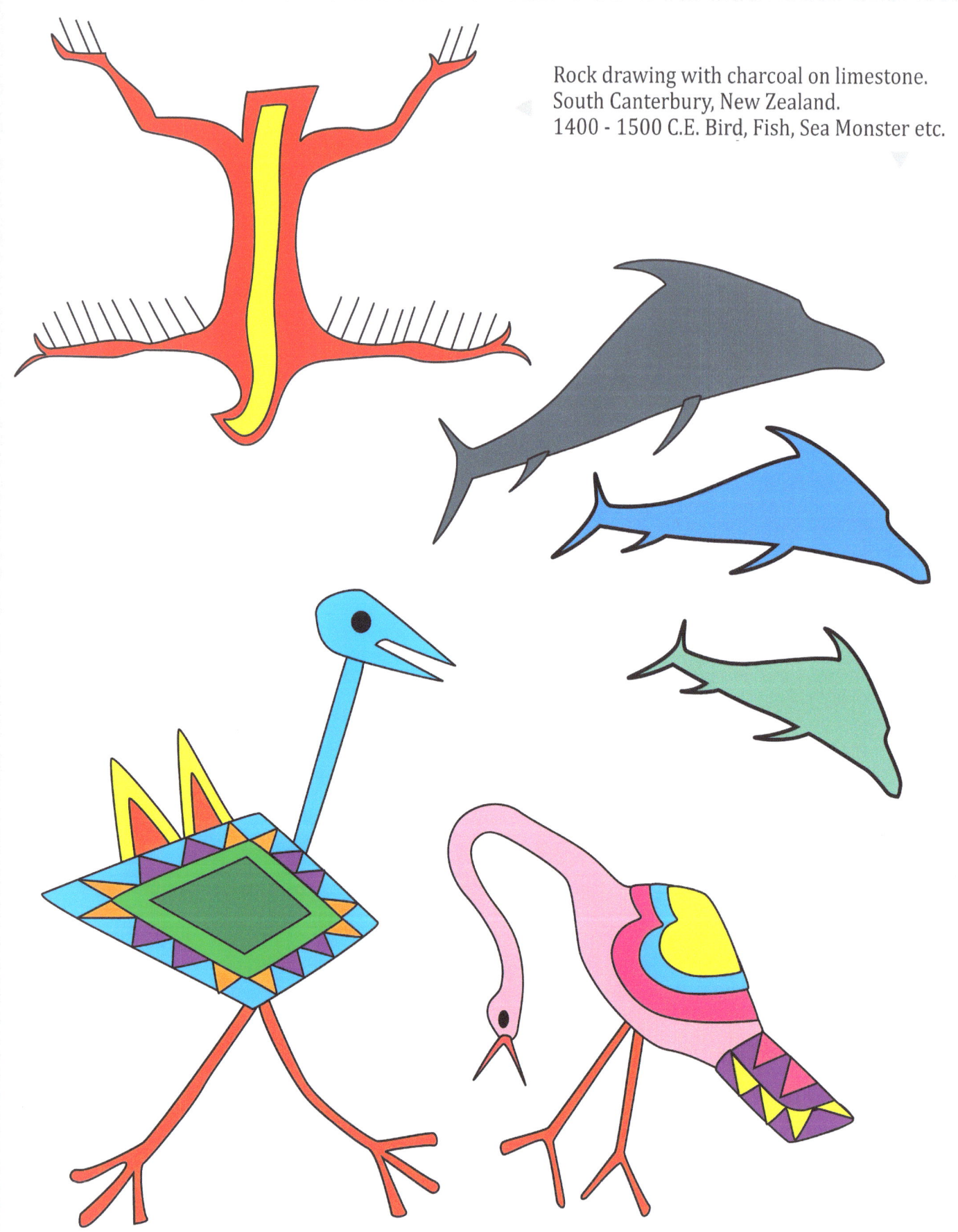

Rock drawing with charcoal on limestone.
South Canterbury, New Zealand.
1400 - 1500 C.E. Bird, Fish, Sea Monster etc.

On a Maori house panel. Relief woodwork. New Zealand.

Oceanic Art

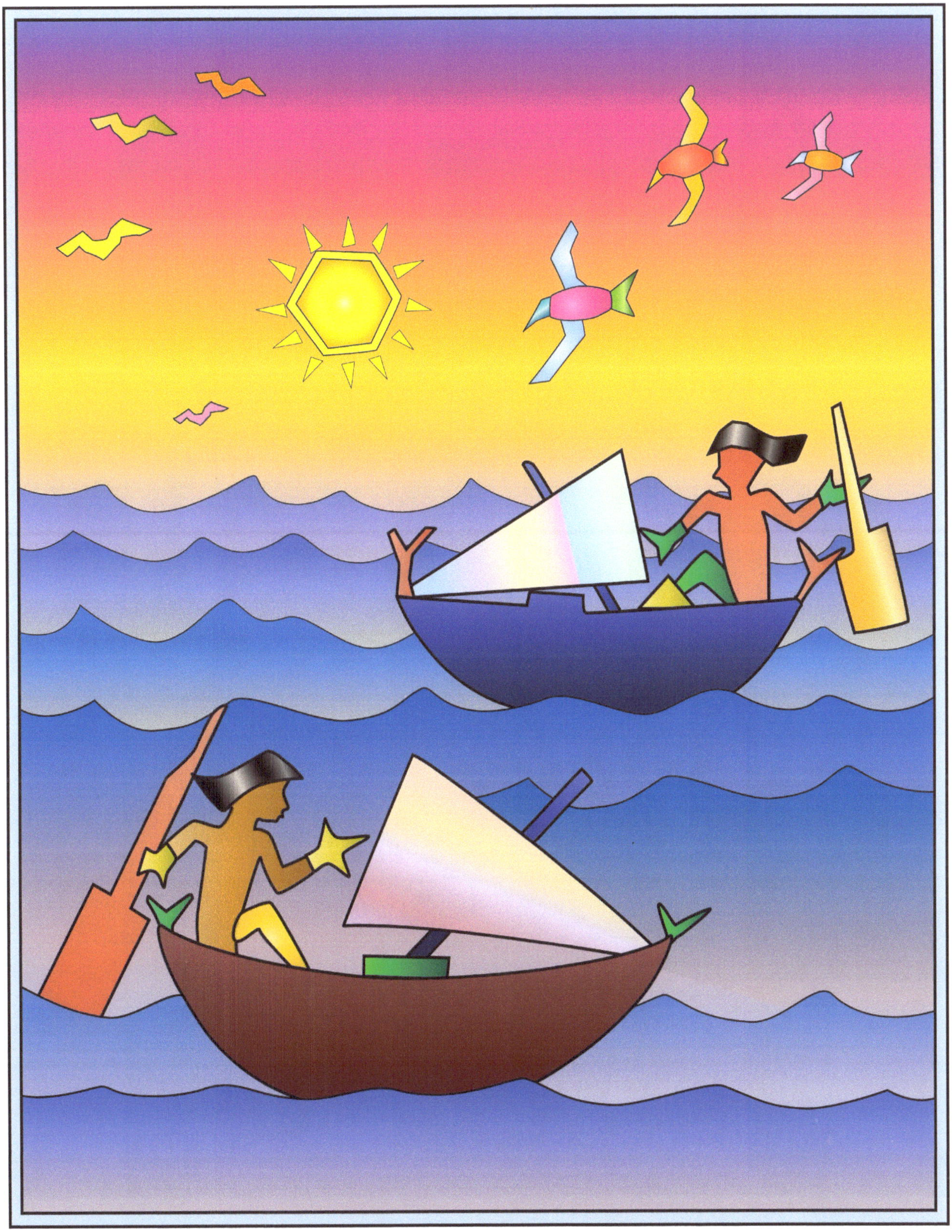

Highly stylized scene from a house panel with relief. Maori woodwork. New Zealand.

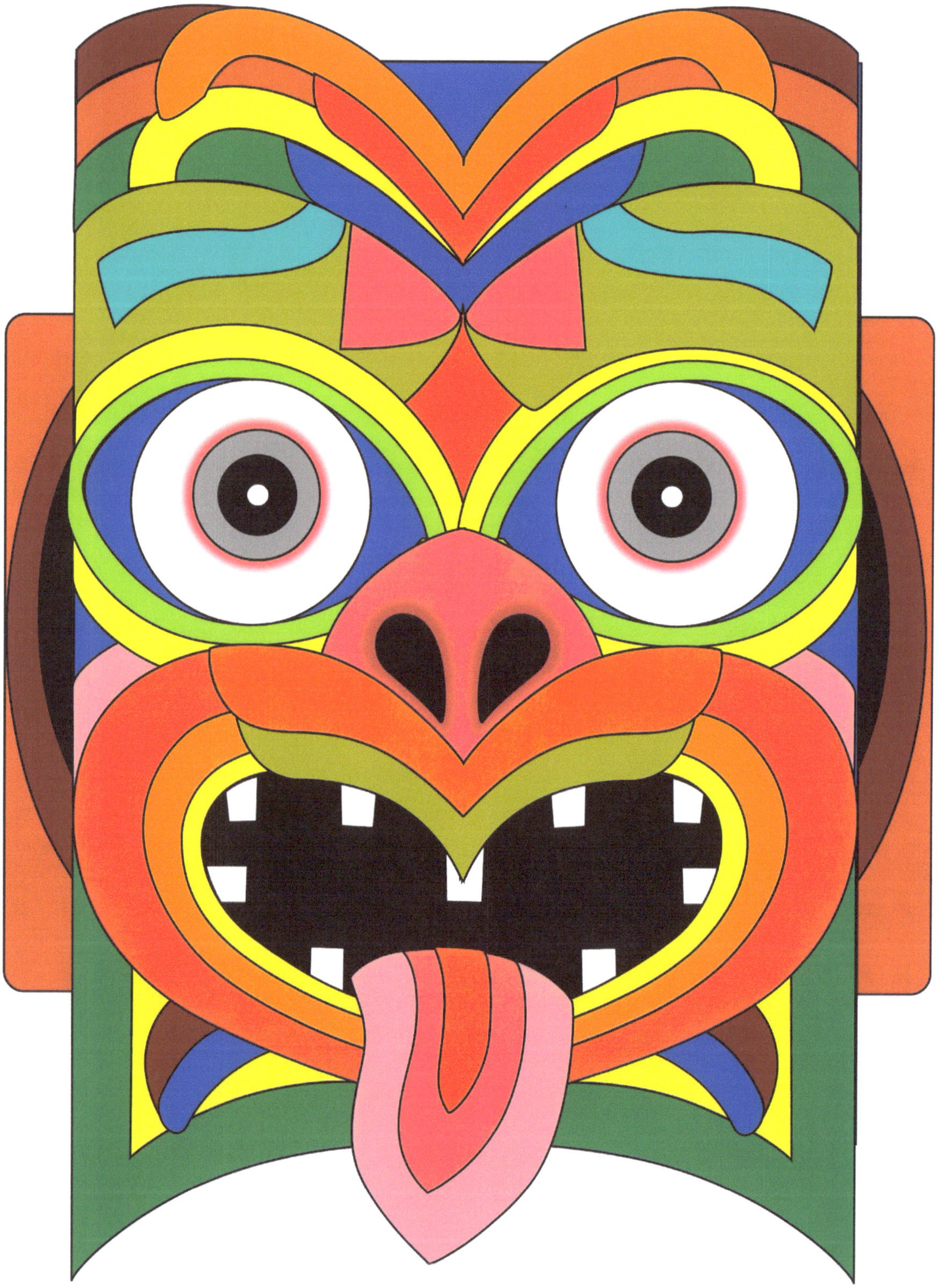

A mask in the pediment of a traditional Maori Haka.

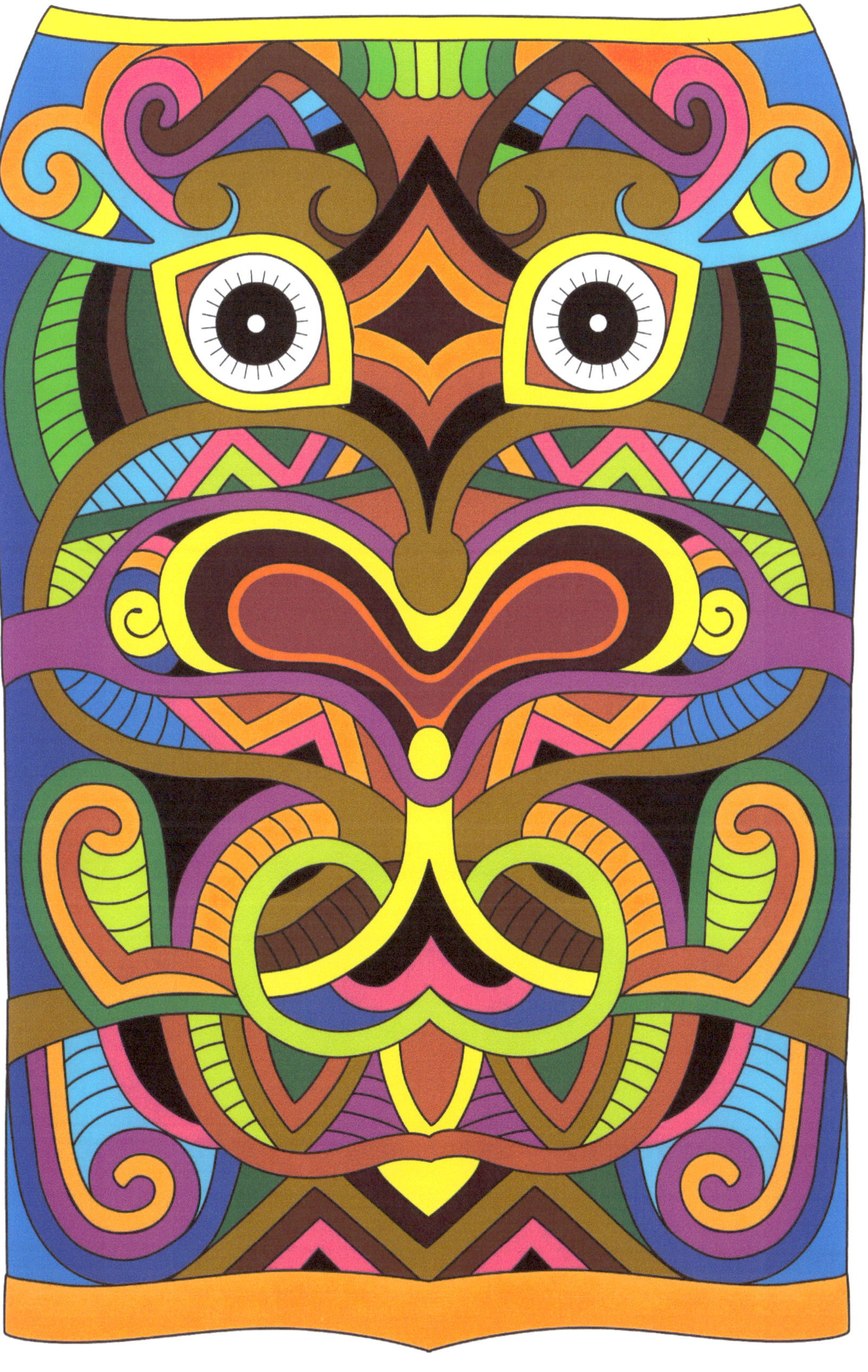

Maori wood carving on wall decoration. New Zealand

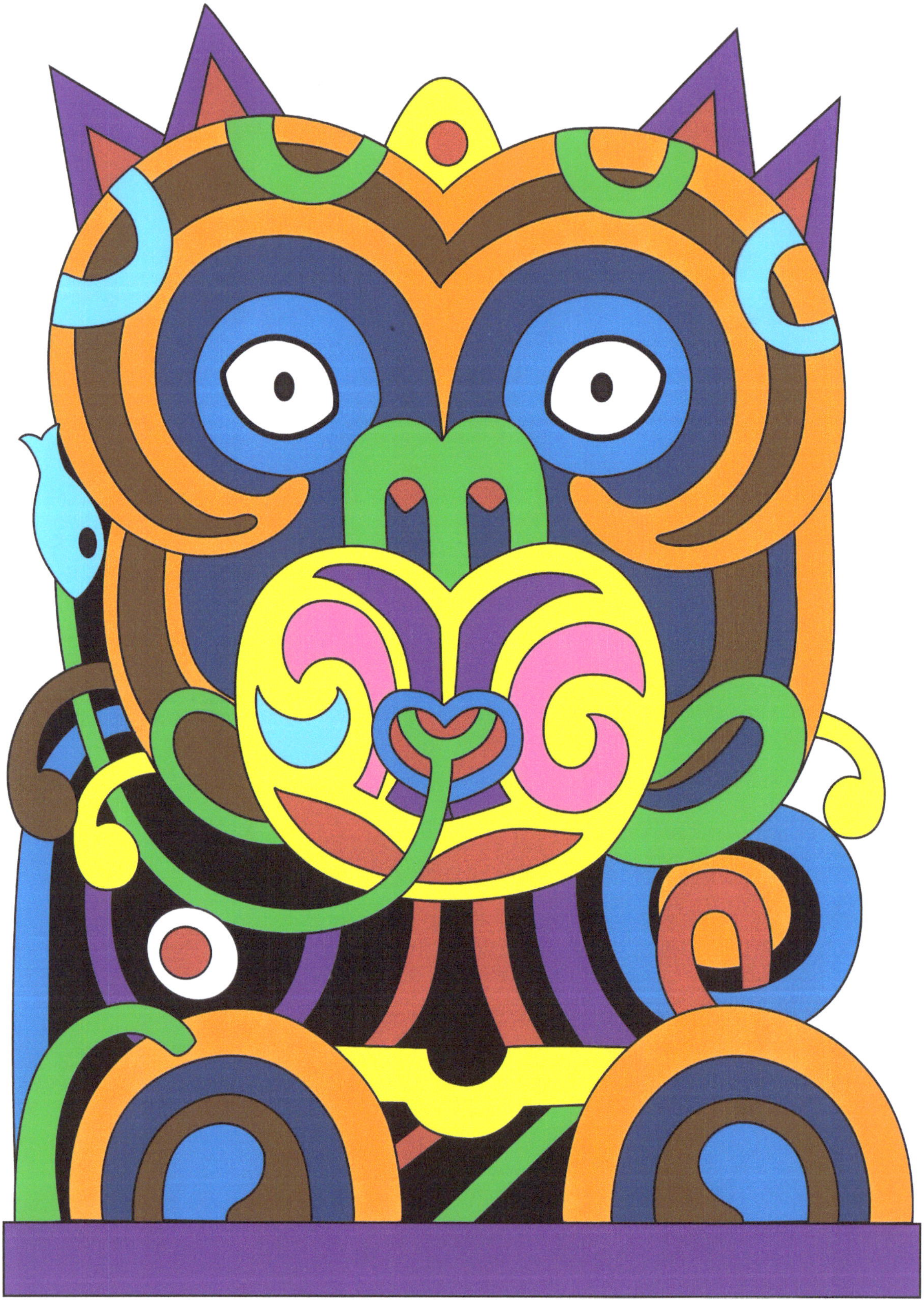

An ancestral panel in Hotunui, a meeting house. Wood carving. The creature is a sea monster of the Thames people. Ureia in the form of a Marakihau.

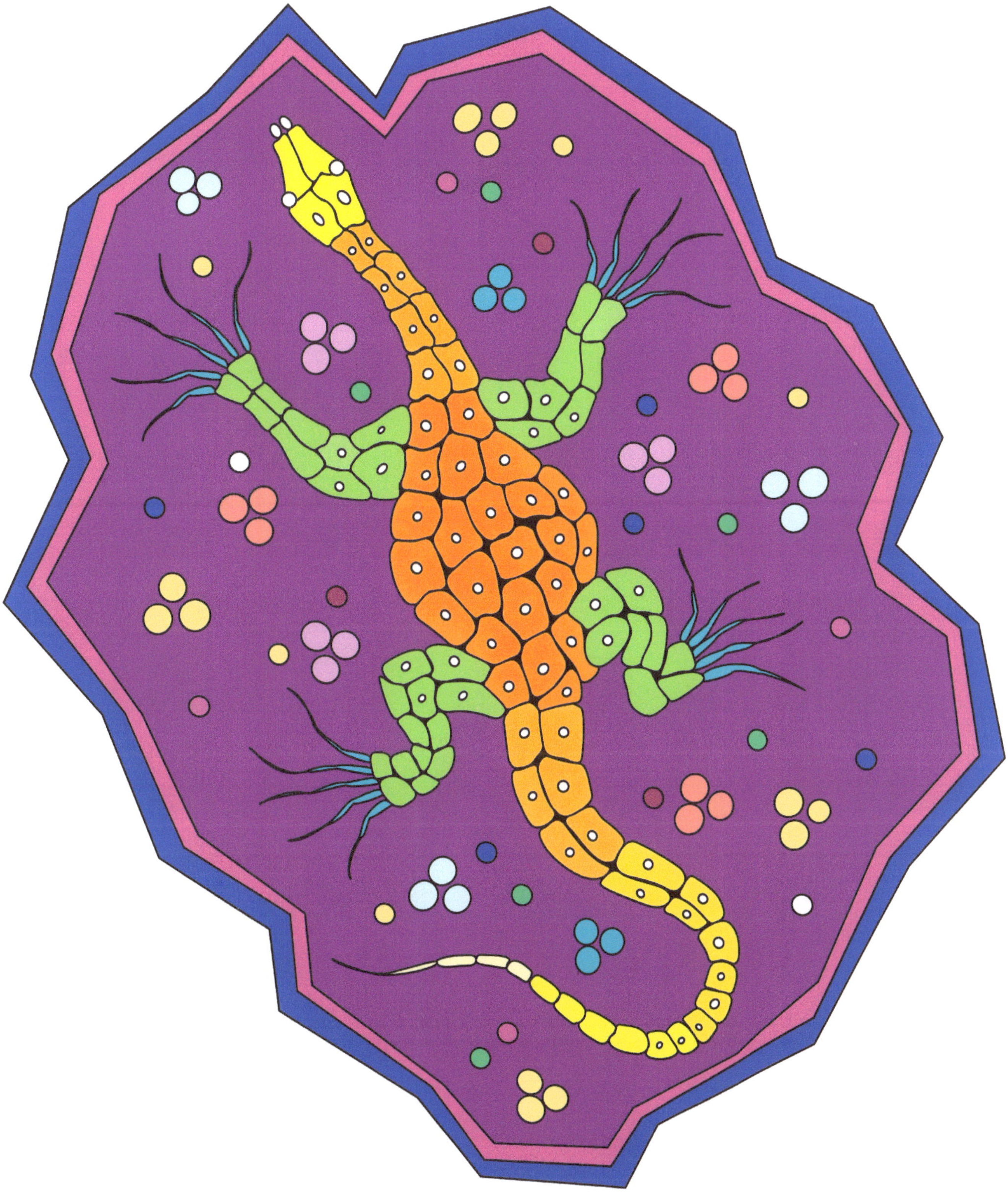

Goanna Dreaming, a myth associated with the dream.
Created by an Australian Aboriginal Artist

27

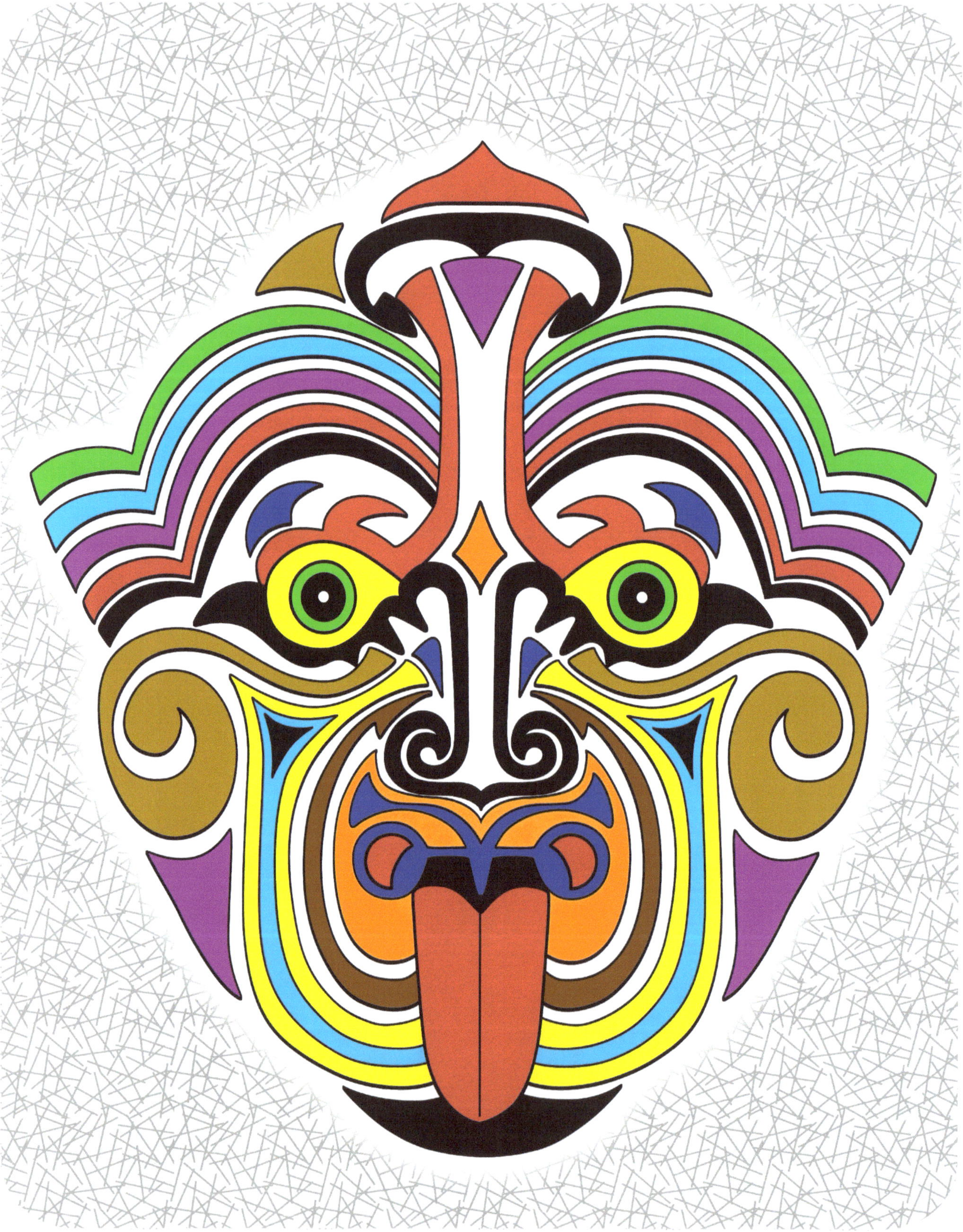

Maori Heads paint on their face to express valor and leadership.

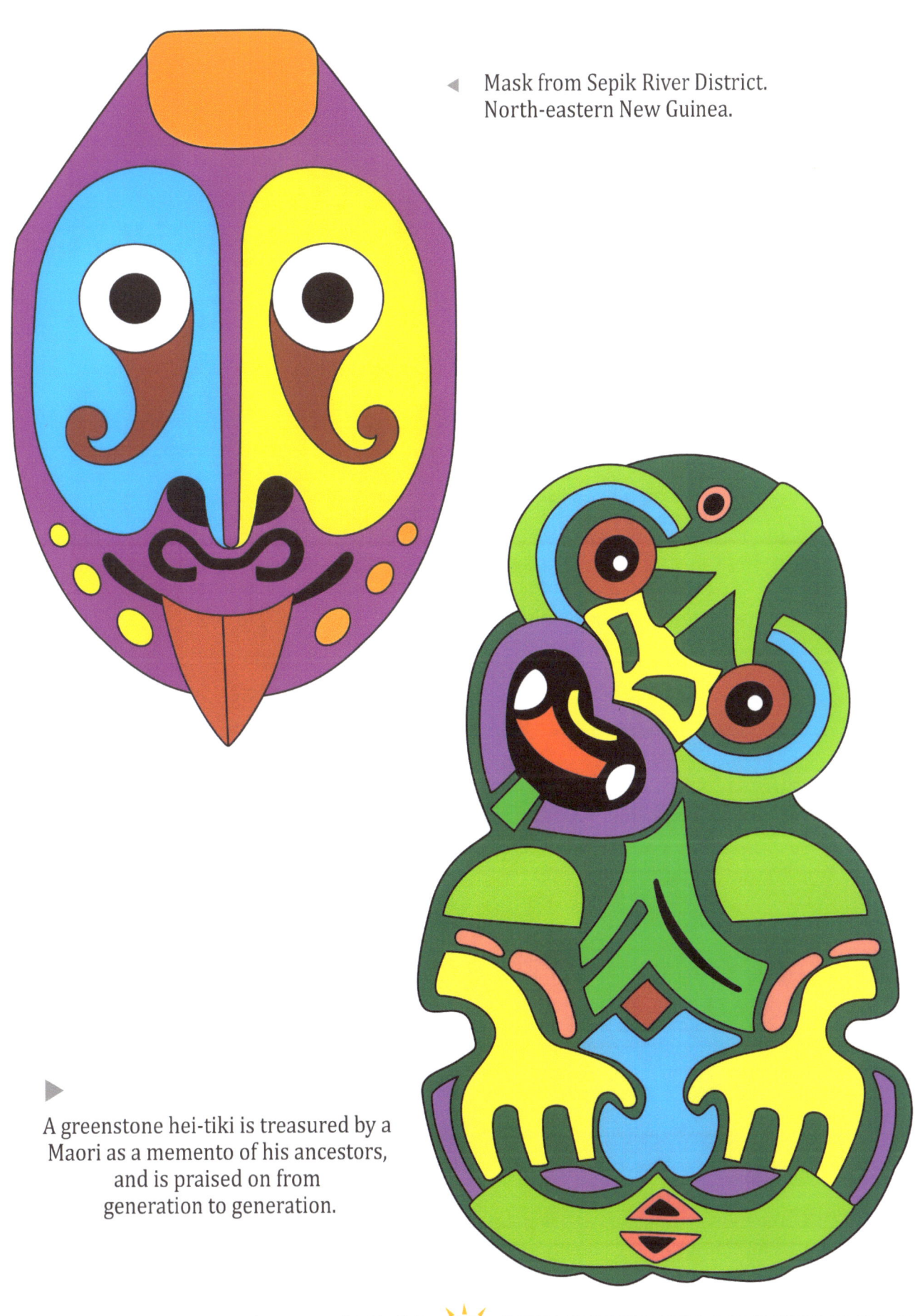

◄ Mask from Sepik River District.
North-eastern New Guinea.

► A greenstone hei-tiki is treasured by a
Maori as a memento of his ancestors,
and is praised on from
generation to generation.

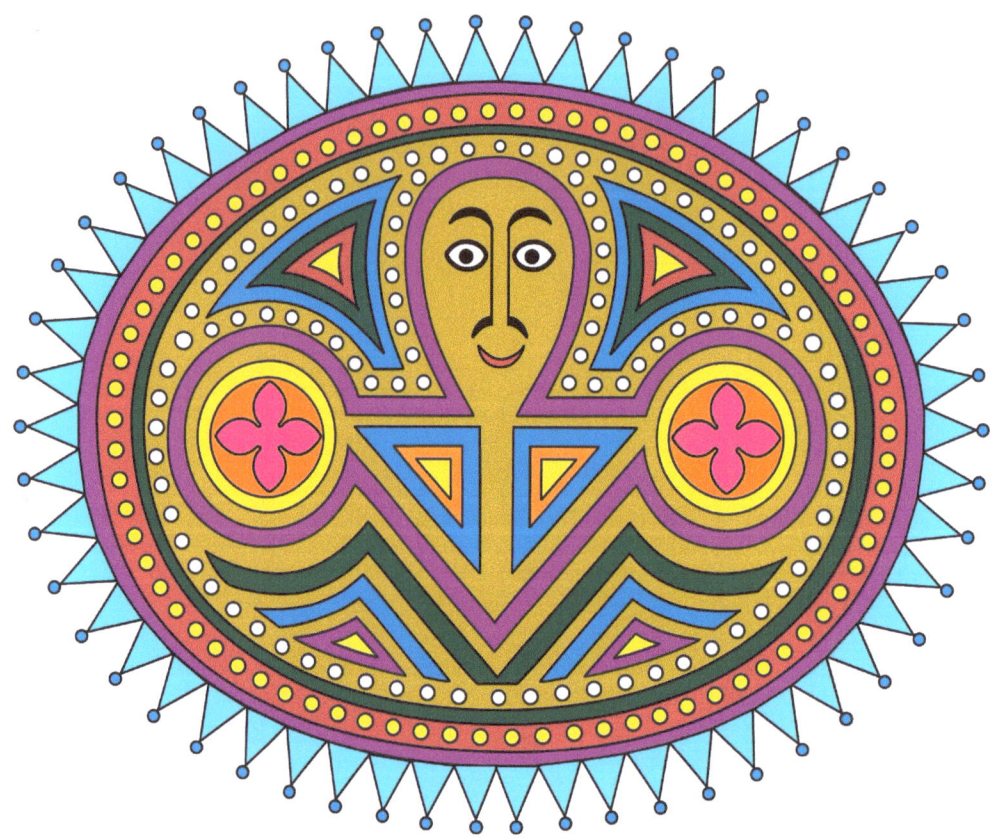

On a Lapita pottery. An anthropomorphic design. 1000 B. C. E.

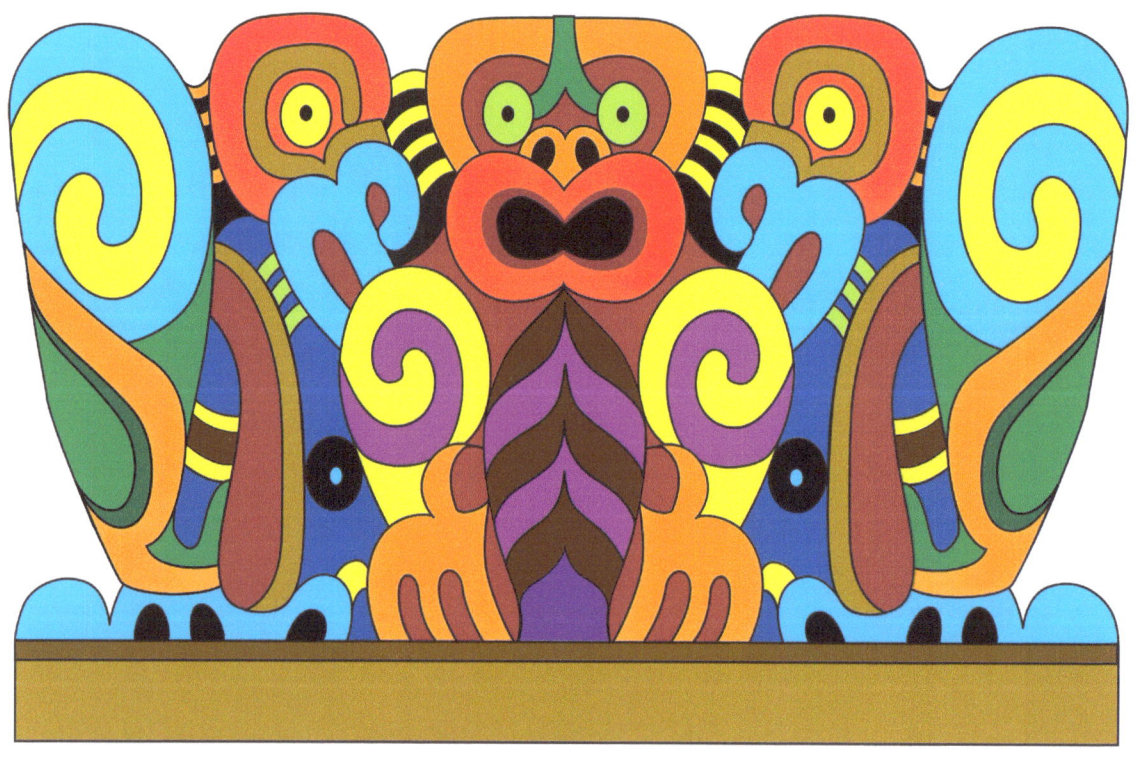

Carving in the Te Puawai O Te Arawa storehouse, New Zealand.
Maoris were extremely creative people. Maori oratory with its frequent reference
to the mythic part, was a highly developed art. Their poetry ranging from sublime
pathos to rowdy humour is some of the most evocative ever composed.

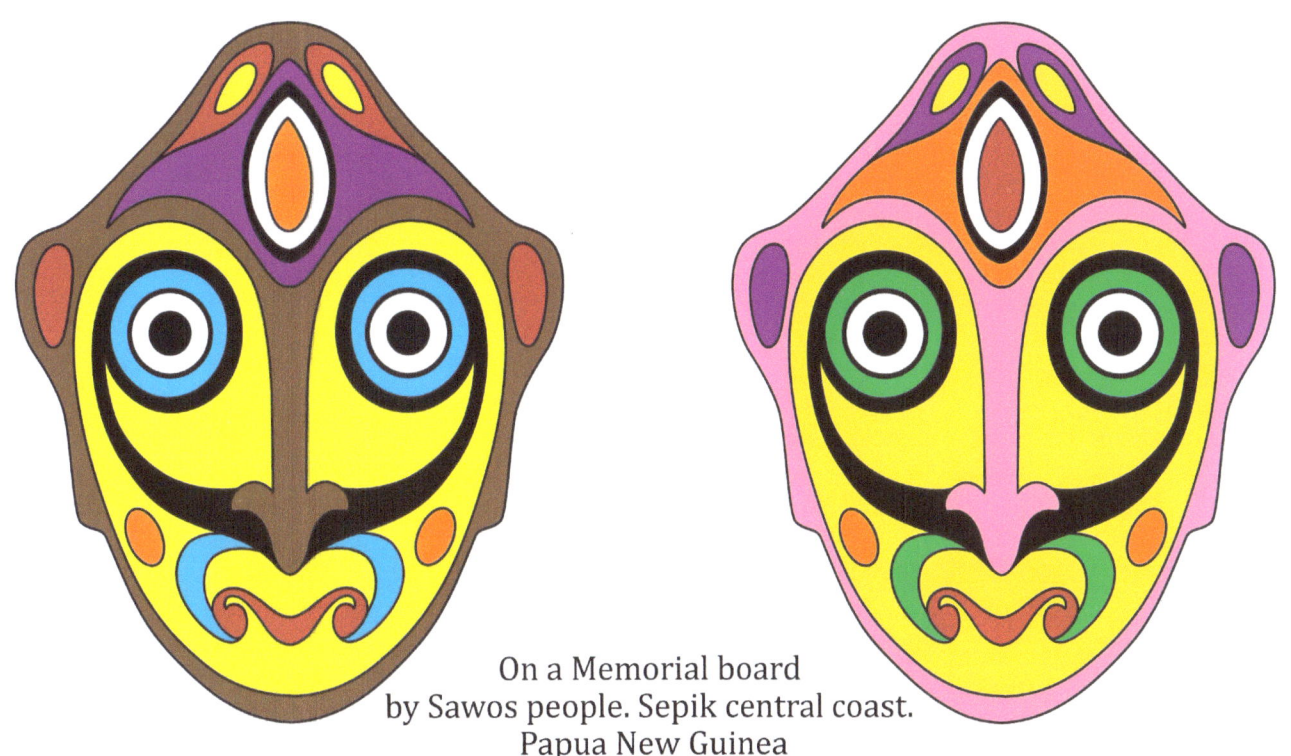

On a Memorial board
by Sawos people. Sepik central coast.
Papua New Guinea

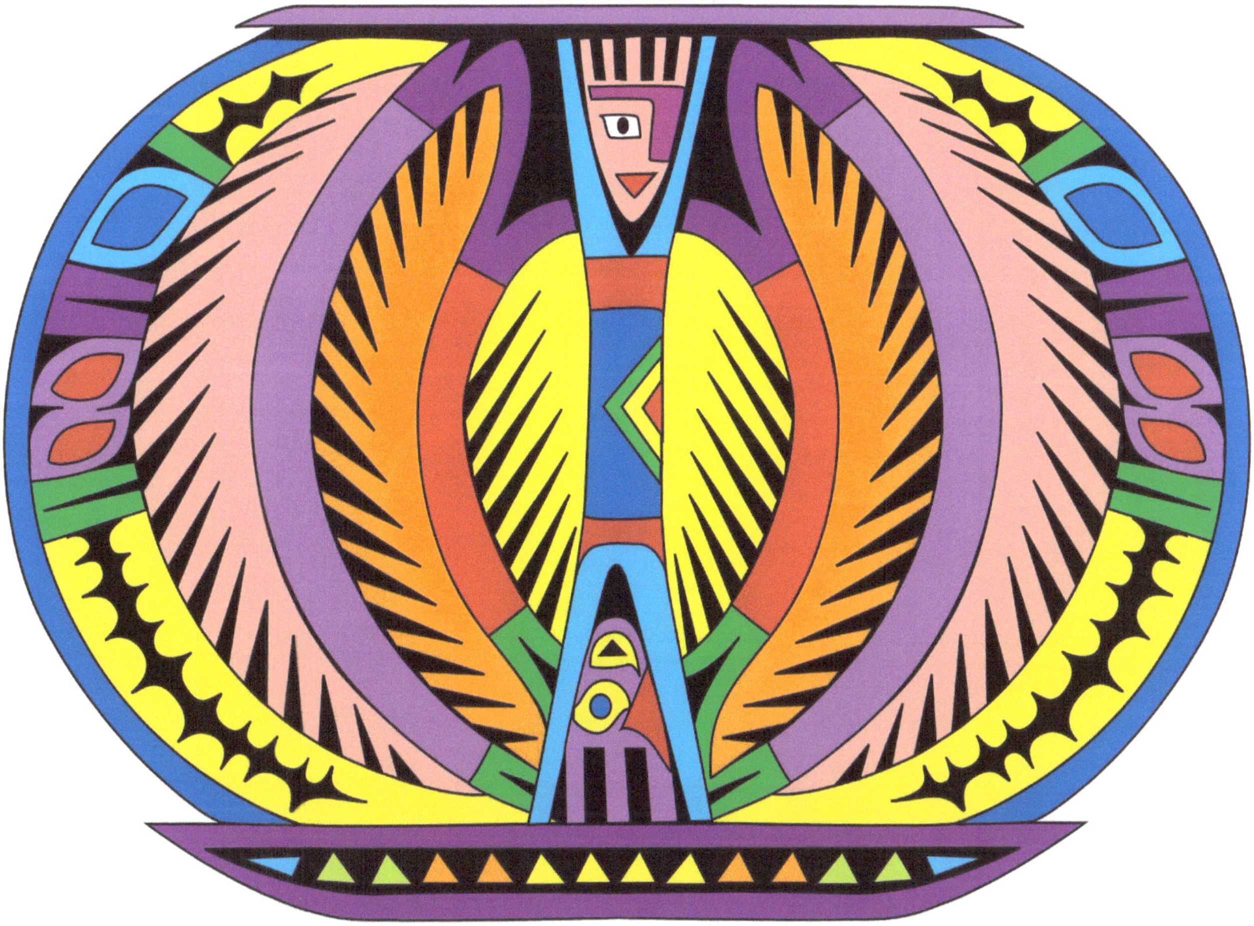

Malanggan from northern New Ireland.
Large openwork carving in soft wood. Usually in the form of a horizontal frieze.

31

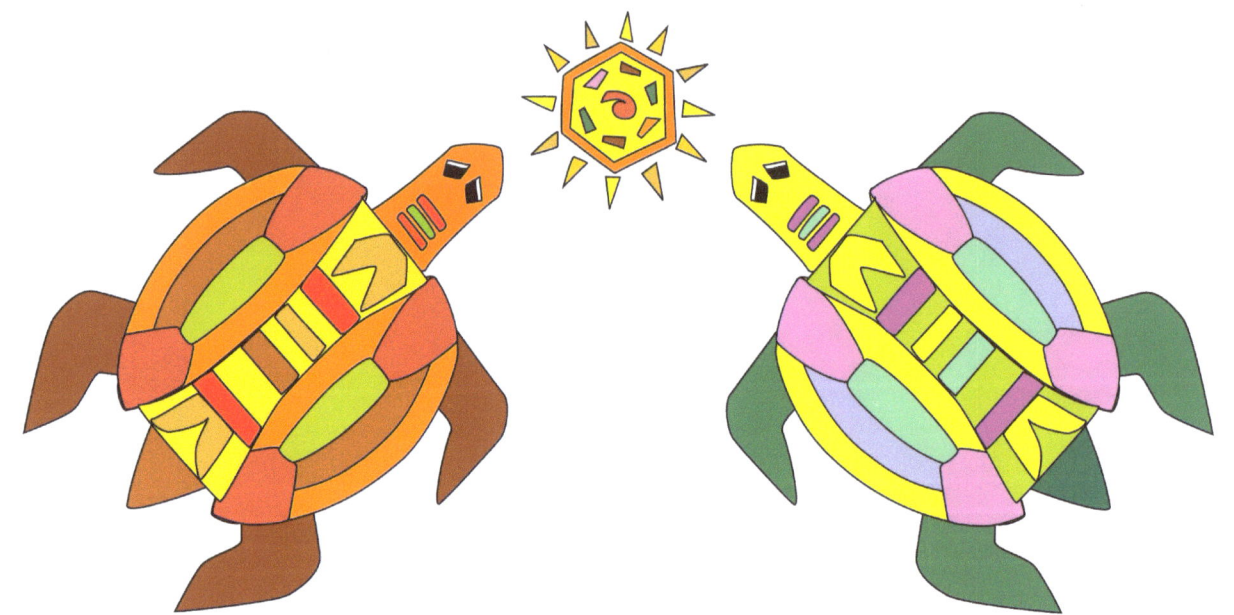

On a Maori house panel. Relief woodwork. New Zealand.

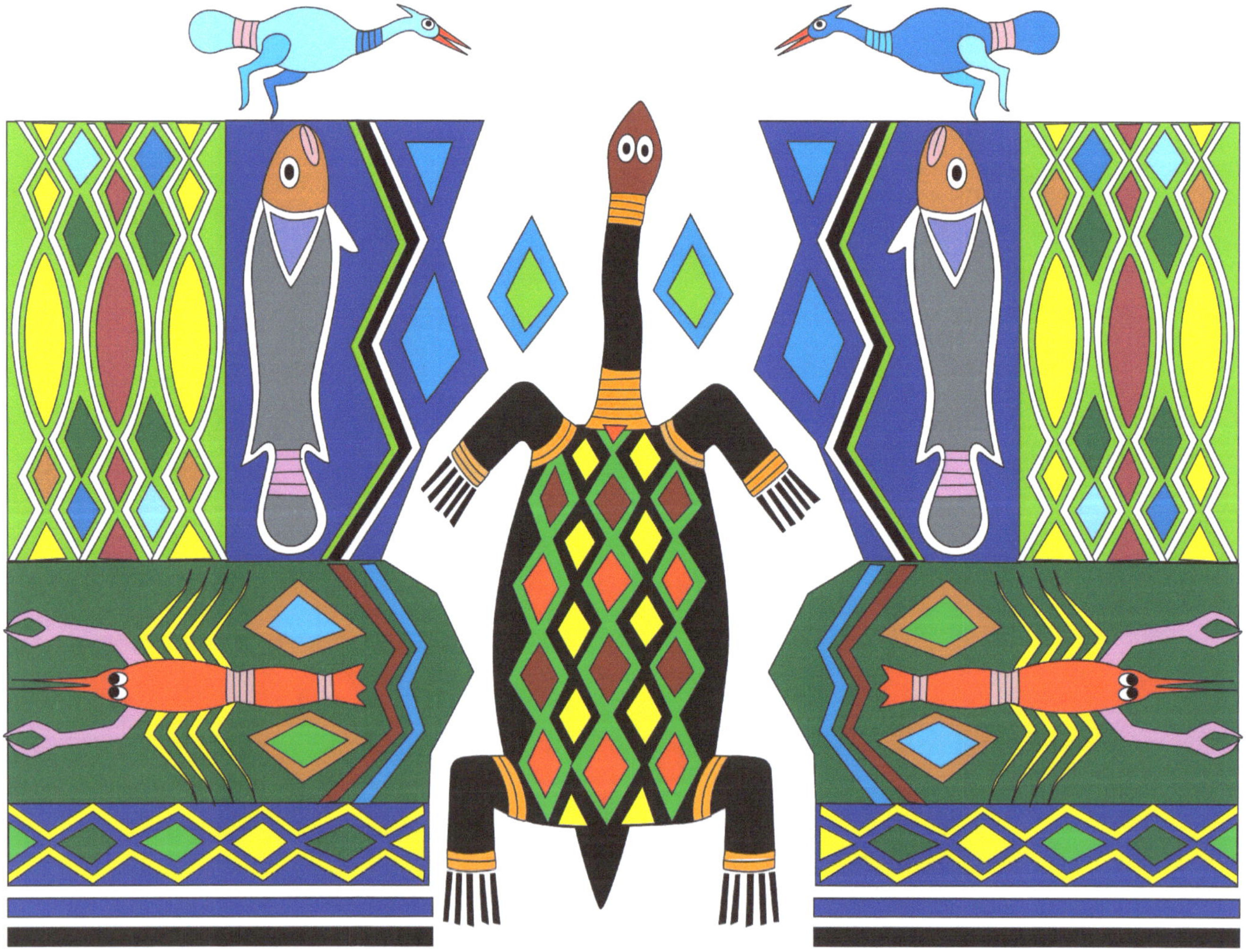

A painting on eucalyptus bark by an Australian Aboriginal artist.

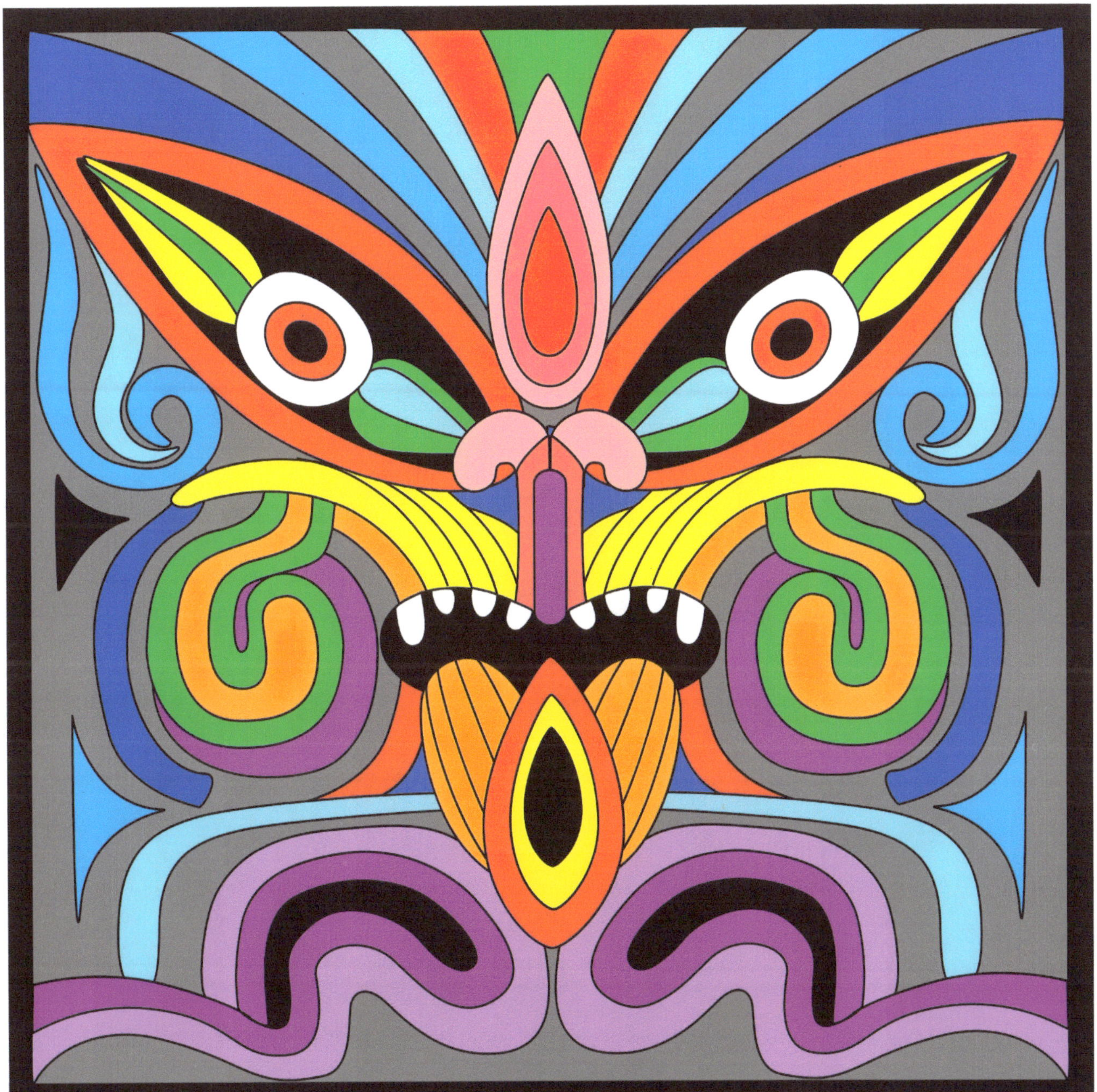

Traditional Maori abstract wall painting, New Zealand.

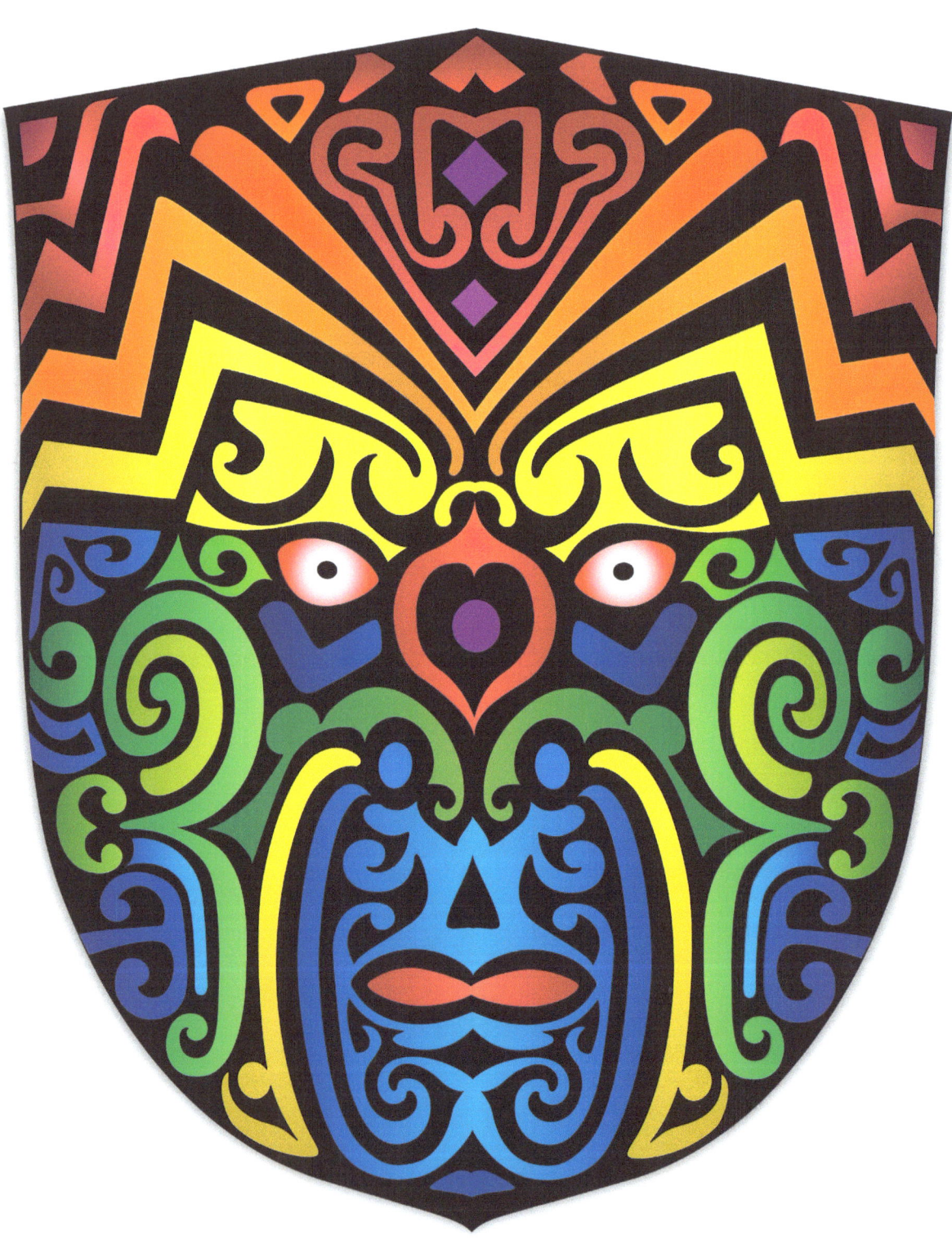

Maori storehouse decoration, wood carving. Showing tattoo on the face of Tama-Te-Kapua, captain of the Arawa canoe from 'Hawaiki,' and legendary founder of the tribe. Carved Wero of Ngati in 1868.

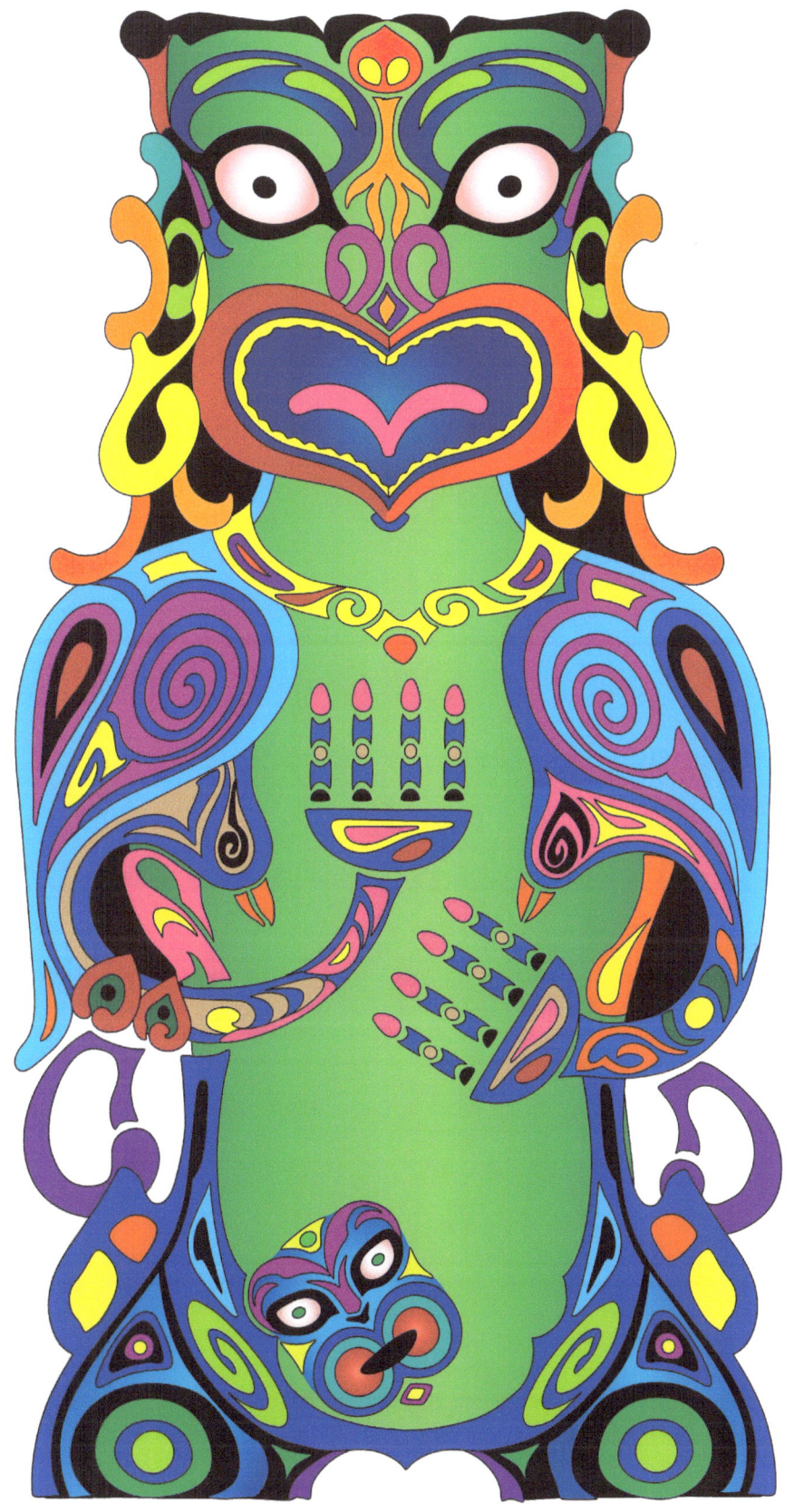

A Chieftain of the Ngati Porou tribe. Maori art. Woodwork, New Zealand. 18th Century C.E.

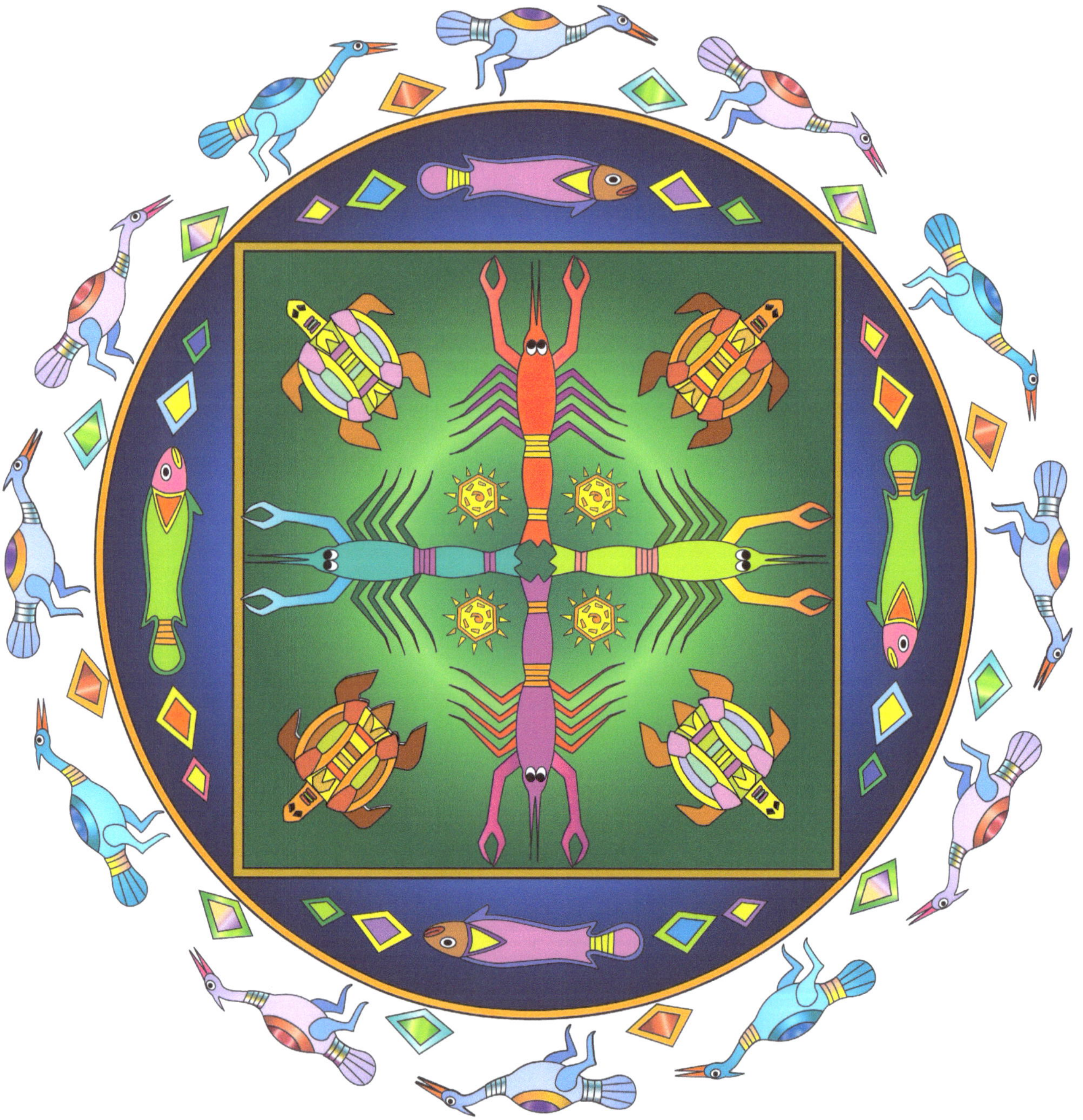

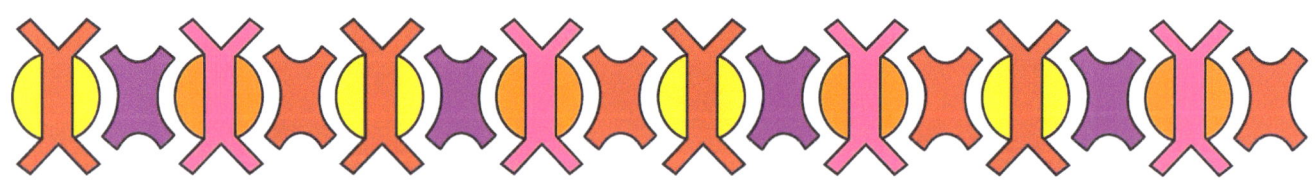

Examples of images created using the elements found in Oceanic Art.

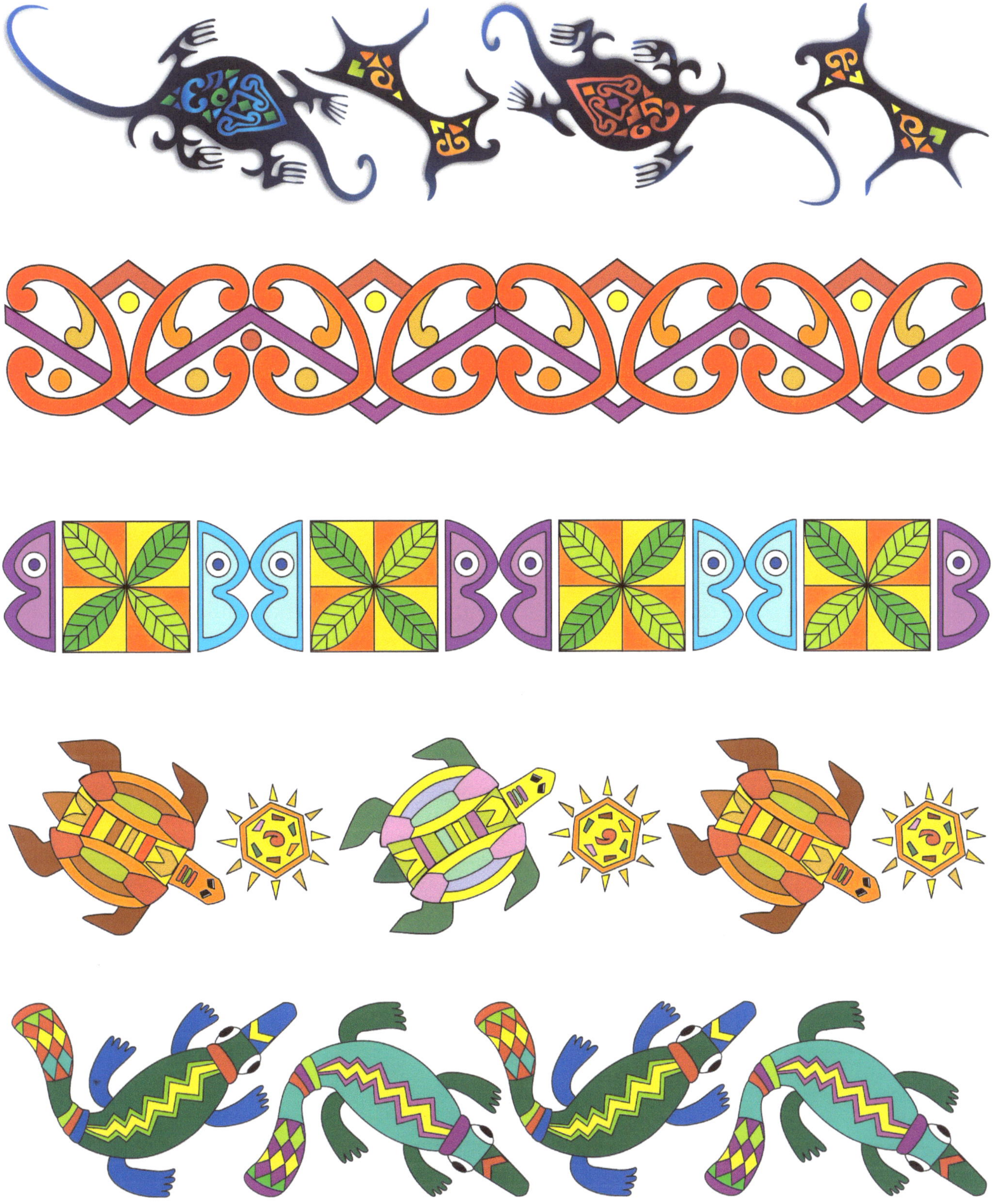

Examples of images created using the elements found in Oceanic Art.

AFRICAN ART

The continent of Africa is filled with vibrant artistic cultures as well as incredible natural beauty. The term African art is typically used for the art of Sub-Saharan Africa. But recently, scholars and art historians have also included the arts of the African Diaspora found in Brazil, the Caribbean, and even in the United States. African Art in its entirety seemingly holds a unifying theme regardless of the diverse cultural differences found within the continent.

Countless of artists and connoisseurs are in awe with admiration of the sculptural qualities African Art possesses. Sculptures have been fashioned using various types of materials found within their local regions. Majority of the sculptures found were created with wood and from blocks of granite. Softer stones were used for carvings in Sierra Leone, Liberia, Yoruba Land, and in Lower Congo regions. Either mud or clay was used for the sculptures that were found on the solid walls.

Craftsmen carved logs into milk pots and other vessels, as well as into stools and headdresses. They even hollowed out tree trunks into canoes and made doors for their huts and granaries out of the thick planks. The art creators carved figurines and masks for religious and social ceremonies. Various forms of African art were made from different materials such as: hematite, sisal, coconut shells, beads, ebony wood, and so forth.

Pottery was customarily a woman's craft in Africa. Water pots and cooking vessels were coiled first and then roughly fired to maintain their shape. The life-size terracotta figures were made by men in northern Nigeria over two thousand years ago.

Tribal masks played an important role in the African indigenous community since the cultures are imbued with spirituality. Masks were worn in a variety of ways for festivals, initiation ceremonies, and secret societies. They were believed to represent a spirit who possessed the wearer.

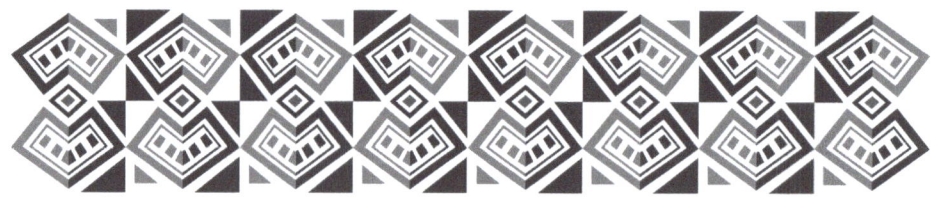

= a synopsis of =

Oceanic Art

The creative works of art produced by the native peoples of the Pacific Island, Australia, as well as the areas as far as Hawaii and Easter Island are referred to as Oceanic art. The term Oceanic art encompasses the tradition of the indigenous to Australia, New Zealand, and the Pacific Islands.

The artistic creations vary throughout the cultures and regions. The focal point of the themes are typically of fertility or the supernatural. Masks created as their art traditionally used in religious ceremonies or social rituals. Tattooing, paintings, wood carvings, and textile work are common forms of Oceanic art. The Oceanic population did not see their work as the western concept of 'Art,' but rather created objects for the practical purpose of use in religious and social ceremonies, or for use in their domestic life.

Australoid people or the ancestors of modern day Melanesians, and Australian Aboriginals travelled there between 40,000 and 60,000 years ago. They did not have a standard writing system and made their works on mostly perishable materials, as a result very few of them exist. By 1500 B.C.E., works of Dong Son culture of Vietnam, known for their Bronze work can be found all over in the Oceania region.

The rock art of Australian Aboriginals is the longest continuously practiced artistic tradition in the world. The rock paintings served several functions. They were used in magic, amusements, and to increase animal population for hunting.

Polynesian art is characteristically ornate, meant to contain supernatural, and flourished after 1600 C.E. Maori culture in New Zealand are known for their Face carving and Tattooing as it was a traditional practice especially by men of rank, but by women as well.

Oceanian artists never had an effort to achieve the classical ideal of Antiquity of Western civilization. Consequently, most of the proportions in their wooden or stone statues are generally erroneous. The head is generally too large for the body, while the body is too large for the legs, but that never deterred anyone. The concept never became fully fixed in Oceania, and often it is an emotional expression rather than an object of decoration made for beauty. Only feelings and religious relevance are all that matter, the region of Ancient Oceania.

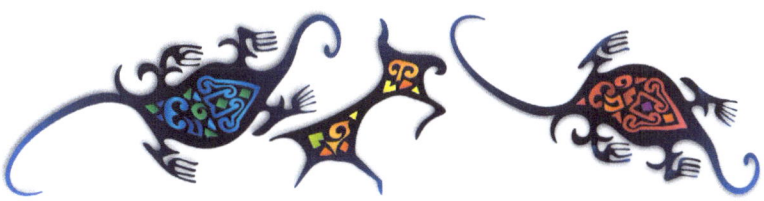

OTHER TITLES IN THIS SERIES

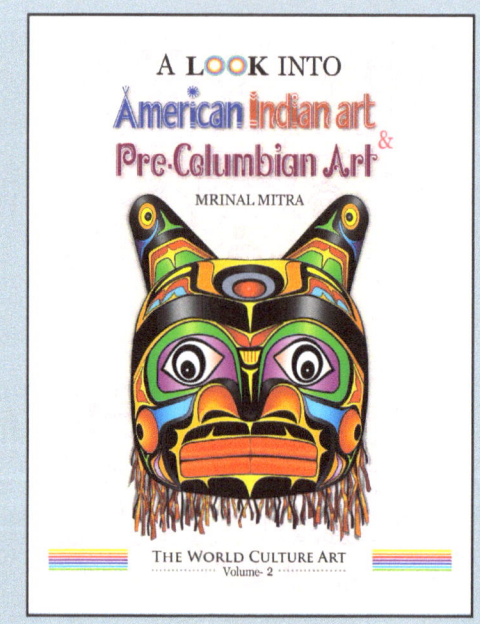

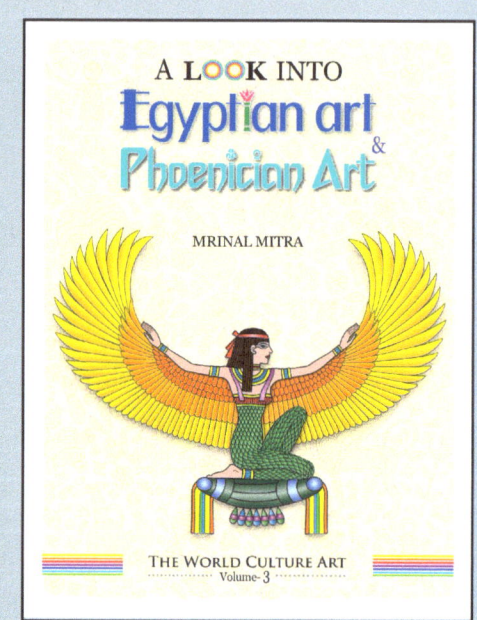

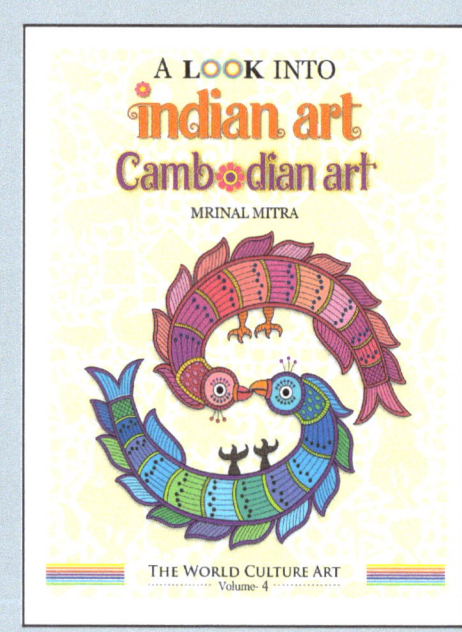

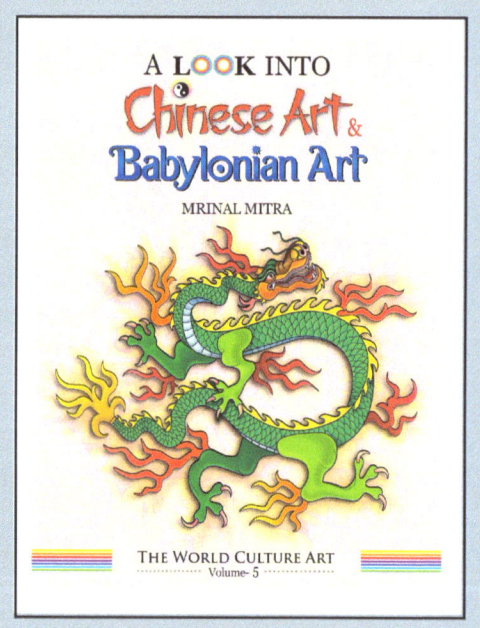

About the Author

Mrinal Mitra has earned a number of prestigious awards, both Indian and International, and received honors for his outstanding illustrations. Some of his recognitions include; The Noma Concours Award (twice), Tokyo, Japan, Illustrators Award, and Children`s Choice Award, India, and Honors from German Television `Transtel`, BRNO- CSSR, and UNICEF, New York, USA.

Many of his talented artworks have been exhibited in various countries such as; India, Japan, Italy, Czech Republic, Iran, and New Zealand. Mitra has authored, designed, and illustrated trades and educational children books for many Indian as well as Multinational Book Publishers around the globe.

Copyright: Mrinal Mitra, 2016

Printed by CreateSpace, an Amazom.com company.
Available from Amazon.com, CreateSpace.com, and other retail outlets.